P9-DHF-177

FOR
SOCCER-CRAZY
GIRLS
ONLY

FOR

SOCCER-CRAZY

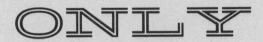

GIRLS

ONLY

ERIN DOWNING

ILLUSTRATED BY
HEADCASE DESIGN

FEIWEL and FRIENDS

NEW YORK

A FEIWEL AND FRIENDS BOOK
An Imprint of Macmillan

Feiwel and Friends books may be purchased for business or promotional use. For information on bulk purchases, please contact the Macmillan Corporate and Premium Sales Department at (800) 221-7945 x5442 or by e-mail at specialmarkets@macmillan.com.

Library of Congress Cataloging-in-Publication Data Available

ISBN: 978-1-250-04709-0

Design and illustrations by Headcase Design

Feiwel and Friends logo designed by Filomena Tuosto

First Edition: 2014

10 9 8 7 6 5 4 3 2 1

mackids.com

ACKNOWLEDGMENTS

Special thanks to Mike Navarre and Marta Fraboni,
soccer-crazy super-editors and great friends. I couldn't have
written this without your advice and guidance.
(Note: Any and all errors are mine alone.)

Thanks also to John Coy and Liz Szabla, for the opportunity
and for your partnership. Also, my sincere thanks to the rest
of the Macmillan crew—you're quite a team!

My year in England wouldn't have been the same without
my friend Rob Skyner, who took me to my first professional
soccer match in Liverpool, and showed me what it means to
be a true football fan. I'll never forget it.

CONTENTS

CONTENTS

TAKING CARE OF YOU: HOW TO EAT LIKE A SOCCER CHAMPION 64

PLAY SAFE: PREVENTING INJURIES ON THE PITCH 56

I WANT TO DO THAT! SOCCER JOBS 72

CONTENTS

ON THE WORLD STAGE 86

INSPIRATIONAL SOCCER 104

CONTENTS

INTRODUCTION

To be a great soccer player, you must be in love with the game. —Mia Hamm

DO YOU LOVE lacing up your cleats for the first game of the season—and do you love it even *more* when they're caked with mud *after* the game? Are there many nights when you dream about kicking the ball, watching as it soars through the air toward the goal? Would your perfect day include hours on the soccer field? Do you love to watch people play, soaking up everything you can from other soccer-crazy players? Have you ever felt like your soccer team is a second family? Then you're definitely soccer-crazy . . . and this book is definitely for you!

Soccer—also called *football* or *fútbol*—is the best and most popular sport in the world. (But I bet you already know that, don't you?) Almost everyone on earth plays soccer at some point in his or her life. People love soccer not just because it's fun—it's also a sport that can be played almost anywhere, so it's easy to get a game going anytime. In fact, many people use plastic bags, bottles, anything, to make a ball. All you need is *something* to kick around, an open patch of ground, and a friend (or a few) and you're good to go.

I still remember the first professional soccer match I ever attended. I was living in England, and after many months of watching English Premier League matches on TV with my roommates, a good friend offered to take me to a Liverpool game. I distinctly remember the passion of the fans in the stadium, and the amazing level of play I saw on the field (which they call a *pitch* in England). I'd never seen soccer like that, and I felt incredible wearing my friend's Liverpool jersey and getting swept up with the rest of the crowd in the thrill of the game. Afterward, we went to the fish and chips shop outside the stadium and cheered for our team with everyone else who swarmed into the streets . . . and I felt like I was a part of something important. That's what soccer does for people: It builds a community and gives you something amazing to believe in. Soccer is all about the power of a team, the power of every player, natural and practiced talent, and the beauty of the game.

I've always loved soccer, and if you're reading this book, I'm guessing you do, too. Inside, you'll find everything you'll ever need or want to know about soccer: fun and strange facts, interesting information about soccer all over the world, training tips to help make you a soccer superstar, and plenty of details about some of the most extraordinary and influential players who ever played the game. This isn't a regular book that needs to be read from front to back. You can start anywhere, and read any section that catches your eye in whatever order you like.

In addition to reading dozens of books and visiting hundreds of websites while I was trying to find the best information to include in *For Soccer-Crazy Girls Only*, I also got great advice and feedback from some very helpful soccer-crazy friends. Dr. Mike Navarre is the head women's soccer coach at Augsburg College in Minneapolis, Minnesota, and he had some extra insights for soccer-crazy girls—you'll find helpful advice and suggestions from Coach Mike throughout the book.

So now dig in to discover absolutely everything you've ever wanted to know about your favorite sport!

BECOMING T·H·E BEST

THE SECRET TO
SOCCER SUCCESS

FOR MANY SOCCER-LOVING GIRLS, the game is all about having a good time— and that's exactly what it should be about!

Most people play soccer because it's the greatest sport in the world, and it's a ton of fun. If you enjoy soccer just because you like getting together to practice or play with a group of friends who you have a great time with, that's awesome.

But some soccer-crazy girls want more than just fun—they want to be one of the best. So what are some of the steps that a *good* soccer player can take to become a *great* soccer player? To be good, you must love to play. That's obvious. The more you enjoy playing soccer, the more often you will play—and, of course, practice (tons and tons of practice), which makes you better. Taking the time to master your sport will make you a much stronger player and will probably lead to you loving soccer even more.

There are many good players out there: women who make trapping or dribbling seem like an art form, or girls who can run for hours and still have that extra burst that will get them through the last hard minutes of a long game.

But what's the difference between those very good players and the greatest players on earth? One of the most important things great players have is competitive spirit, the fire to win that gives them the passion and drive they need to overcome all obstacles. Great players keep their spirits high, even when they're going into a difficult match or coming off a losing streak. They don't give up—ever!

Great players also work very hard. They use up every bit of energy at practice, and push themselves to learn and master every aspect of their sport. In her fascinating autobiography and soccer guide, *Go for the Goal: A Champion's Giude to Winning in Soccer and Life*, Mia Hamm shares something memorable her legendary coach, Anson Dorrance, noted while she was college: **"The vision of a champion is someone who is bent over, drenched in sweat, at the point of exhaustion when nobody else is watching."** Mia and her teammates practiced—as a team, and as individuals—until they didn't have an ounce of energy left in their bodies. That's how they became the best.

If you want to become a truly great player and a soccer champion, you need to focus on soccer almost like it's a full-time job. In many ways, exceling at sports is even harder than working most jobs because of how much time you have to put in to them, and how hard you have to perform.

Remember, you are the only person who can make greatness happen for yourself. It's *your* body and *your* mind, and you have to make them both work hard. Practice both with your team and alone, prepare for the situations you'll encounter on the field, and get tough—mentally and physically. That's how to follow in the footsteps of some of the best players in the world.

To watch people push themselves further than they think they can, it's a beautiful thing. —Abby Wambach

THE
FOUR
ELEMENTS
OF SOCCER

THERE ARE FOUR basic elements that work in harmony to make up the game of soccer: technical, tactical, physical, and psy- cholocial. All four are essential to your success on the field, and they're all aspects you'll continue to work to improve throughout your soccer career. We'll talk in more detail about each of these elements throughout the next few sections.

If you don't let something break you, you're going to come out stronger in the end. —Hope Solo

TECHNICAL

These are basic skills such as passing, receiving, shooting, playing the ball in the air, and dribbling. Technical skills can be improved through practice, practice, and more practice!

PHYSICAL

The physical elements of soccer include things like speed, strength, agility, and overall fitness (this includes nutrition, too).

TACTICAL

You begin to develop your tactical skills— understanding game strategy and how to play "smart"—as you become a more advanced player. Tactical skills will develop over time and with more exposure to the game.

PSYCHOLOGICAL

People often talk about "mental tough-ness"—this is your ability to get up and stay strong in the face of adversity and difficult situations. The psychological element of soccer is also about having a positive attitude, the will to win, and the motivation to improve.

TRAINING ON YOUR OWN

T HE BEST WAY to get better is to play as often as you can, and to always look for opportunities to improve. That means always attending practices with a good attitude, doing your best to learn from watching others, and working hard on fundamental skills when you're at home, practicing on your own.

Coach Mike says: "You don't have to be on a team to play soccer. You can play in your backyard or your basement and work on your ball skills in the off-season. Pretend you're scoring goals to win the World Cup. Self-motivation is going to help make you one of the best."

SOME BASIC DRILLS YOU CAN DO ON YOUR OWN INCLUDE

- kicking a ball into a net to practice your shooting
- practicing passing and throw-ins against the wall of a building or the side of your garage
- organizing small pickup games with neighborhood friends or a parent
- playing keep-away with your dog or a friend to work on agility
- juggling
- heading practice

O NE OF THE MOST important skills you can learn as a soccer player is how to juggle a soccer ball with your feet. Juggling will help you with dribbling and agility—important technical and physical skills.

When learning how to juggle the ball, the biggest mistakes a beginner makes is not "locking" her ankle and forgetting to keep her big toe down. The secret to success-fully juggling a ball is a combination of (1) concentration, (2) keeping the ball low to the ground, and (3) staying calm.

Then practice, practice, practice!

Coach Mike says: "You should try to use as many body parts as possible in practicing juggling because it will help improve your overall ball control and ability to handle balls in the air. However, the majority of your time should be devoted to juggling with your feet, because that's what you will use the most when you play."

HEAD IT!

SOMETIMES, THE BALL will come flying straight at you through the air. You can either step to the side and let someone else take control, or you can meet it head on . . . literally. There are a couple of things to keep in mind when you practice stopping or passing the ball with your head:

Use your forehead. Hitting the ball with the top of your forehead will give you the best power and more control. It won't hurt. As long as you're hitting the ball with the right part of your head, you're not going to get a goose egg. Keep your eyes open and your mouth closed. You need to see the ball that's coming at you so you can hit it properly. But keep that mouth closed up tight so you don't bite your tongue.

Lock your neck and keep your back nice and loose. Most of the power from a header doesn't come from your neck or head popping forward (ouch!)—it comes from the power you can get from arching and snapping your upper body. Keep your chin in. This will help you release your neck muscles when you move into the ball.

GO FOR THE GOAL

Somewhere behind the athlete you've become and the hours of practice and the coaches who have pushed you is a little girl who fell in love with the game and never looked back . . . play for her. —Mia Hamm

Mia Hamm's excellent autobiography and soccer guide, *Go for the Goal,* is a must-read for soccer-crazy girls. The book is filled with inspiring stories from Hamm's youth, excellent insider tips (and photos) to help with technique and exercises for training at home, and behind-the-scenes stories from Hamm's years on the US Women's National Team.

ATTENTION

GOALKEEPERS!

A GOALKEEPER'S BEST DEFENSE against a shot on goal is to catch it. The most effective way to catch the ball when you're in the net is to put your hands up with your fingers spread wide and the tips of your thumbs close together—so your hands look like a big W. Using the W, there's almost no chance the ball will squeeze through your hands to knock you on the nose or slip into the net.

Sometimes the shot may be coming at you too hard or too fast to allow you to catch it, so in this case you can punch it. A double-fisted punch is most effective if the ball is coming right at you, but if it's coming at you from the side, a single punch is your most effective weapon.

ROBOKEEPER

HOW WOULD YOU like to try to score against a goalkeeping machine? Did you know there's one called RoboKeeper, which is a special robot goalkeeper that has two cameras for eyes? The robot goalkeeper's eyes take ninety pictures per second, and can follow the ball's path from the penalty line to the goal. The information about the ball gets sent to the robot's motor control, telling the RoboKeeper which way to go to defend the shot. All of this communication happens in less than the 0.3 seconds it takes for a ball to make it from the goal line to the net.

SOCCER TRICKS

STUNTS ON

WHEN YOU'RE TRAINING at home, there are a few flashy moves you can practice working on to really challenge yourself. Of course, mastering basic technical skills is the most important thing a young player can do—but who doesn't want to try a few cool moves from time to time, too? Step-by-step guides for doing some of these moves can be found on eHow.com, and there are a lot of great instructional videos on YouTube as well.

BICYCLE KICK:

Also called a "scissor kick," this is an incredibly difficult move to perform! You need to be able to throw your body up into the air, then kick one leg in front of the other (usually up above the level of your head) without your arms or body touching the ground. A bicycle kick can be executed backwards or sideways. Bicycle kicks take tremendous strength and agility—and a whole lot of trial and error when you're learning how to do them.

FRONT HANDSPRING THROW-IN:

A front handspring throw-in literally involves doing a front handspring toward the touchline with the ball in your hands. You begin your throw-in fifteen to twenty feet away from the side of the field, then take a few steps toward the touchline to give you some momentum for executing a handspring. When you land on your feet again, the force of your handspring will help you throw the ball even further onto the field. Practice regular front handsprings first, and once you've mastered that you can try doing a handspring with the ball in your hands.

THE PITCH

THE RAINBOW:

One of the most famous and flashy moves in soccer, the Rainbow, is also a move that is rarely performed successfully. To do the Rainbow, you step over the ball while you're running forward. Then the ball rolls up your heel, and you flick the ball up and over your head with your leg. If you manage to do it correctly, the ball will fly forward over you, making an arc that looks like a rainbow, before landing on the ground in front of you.

THE MARADONA:

The Maradona is also called the Marseille turn, but is more often referred to as the Maradona because of Diego Maradona, the legendary player who performed the move with great grace and skill. The Maradona is a really cool way to execute a turn—where both you *and* the ball change direction—in order to defend the ball in your possession against an oncoming attacker.

There are three basic steps to a beginner's Maradona move. first, you step lightly on the ball with your dominant foot to stop its forward progress. While that foot is resting gently on the ball, you use your other foot to propel your body to begin its spin to face the other direction. Switch to put your weaker foot on the ball, and continue to spin until you're facing the exact opposite direction you'd been running just a moment before. Then flick the ball forward with your foot to get it moving again.

SOCCER CAMP

ONE GREAT WAY TO immerse yourself in the world of soccer for a week or two is to attend a soccer camp in the summer or during a school break. Many cities and towns around the United States run camps that are staffed by high school or college players, professional coaches, or for a lucky few, professional soccer players.

At these camps, instructors will run drills and work on fundamentals, while focusing on fun, fun, fun. Soccer camp is a great place to meet other soccer-crazy girls who live in your area who play for other teams and leagues.

If you're interested in attending a soccer camp, ask your coach for suggestions, or ask the athletic director at a local high school for recommendations. If you can't find a camp in your area, you could even consider teaming up with some of your friends to start your own. Talk to a few older players, and see if they'd be interested in spending a few afternoons working with you on drills and skills. Or, you could run some fun mini-camps in your yard or at a local park for some of the younger soccer players in your neighborhood—sometimes teaching others is the best way to get better yourself.

SELECT TEAMS

ARE THEY FOR YOU?

IF YOU'RE THINKING about trying out for a select (or "travel") team, there are some things you need to know. Competitive leagues and travel teams require a lot more than just exceptional soccer skills—they take sacrifice, time, and a whole lot of hard work.

Some soccer-crazy girls are perfectly happy to be playing on their rec or school team, but others want year-round play. They want the chance to live and breathe soccer day in and day out. They can't imagine spending their afternoons and evenings doing anything *other* than soccer. Their weekends are spent playing games and tournaments, and their weeknights are spent training. Some might even go so far as to say that they don't mind missing parties and sleepovers and school events for games, since soccer matters more to them.

If you think being on a select team is for you, make sure you talk to your family about it. After all, someone's going to have to drive you around to your games and practices—so you're going to need their support!

Coach Mike says: "Please understand that if you decide to play for a select team, it's a much greater commitment than playing for a recreational team in your neighborhood. Your coach will expect you to be able to practice year-round, and to make soccer a priority."

HOW TO

STAND OUT

AT TRYOUTS

S O YOU'VE DECIDED to try out for a select team. Congratulations! When the big day arrives, how can you make sure you get noticed as someone the coaches would want on their team?

- Be early! Many times, coaches will be keeping their eye on warm-ups, too. And even if they aren't watching warm-ups, if you get there a little early to kick around a ball with a parent or a friend, you'll be ready to go by the time tryouts begin.
- Speak up! Often at tryouts, you'll be playing with a team of girls you've never played with before. Communicate effectively with your new team by letting them know if you or someone else is open, alerting a teammate if someone is running for a pass, or sharing any other important information with your teammates. Also, remember to encourage good plays and be supportive of the players around you. Coaches want leaders, and great communicators are the best leaders.

- Do your best! It's essential that you give it your all at tryouts. This isn't the time to sit back and let others shine—you need to give one hundred percent and then some, since you've only got one chance to win the coaches over. Go after the ball, and then do something with it—whether that *something* is dribbling it up the field to take a shot, passing it to an open teammate, or keeping it out of the net. Play well, play fair, and be supportive of the other people playing out there with you.
- Stay positive! If you lose the ball, hustle to get it back or make yourself useful elsewhere on the field. Don't pout, shout, or get angry. Soccer moves fast, so you've

got to bounce back from mistakes quickly or you'll risk being left behind.
- Stand out! Obviously, great playing is the best way to stand out. But there are other ways to be memorable, too. Perhaps you could wear a pair of wildly colorful socks, do something interesting with your hair, or wear a crazy jersey. If you're more noticeable, you might be more memorable. Of course, you've got to play well, too—cool outfits alone aren't going to win anyone over.

Coach Mike says: "Sometimes, there may be many players trying out for your position—you may increase your chances of making a team if you can play multiple positions."

TRYOUTS

T HE TRYOUTS FOR most select (competitive or traveling) teams will involve some basic technical drills (dribbling through cones, etc.) and some small games or scrimmages (often five-on-five). The coaches will be watching everything—and looking for the best players to include on their roster. So make sure you play hard every minute you're on the field, and show them what you can do. That doesn't mean you need to hog the ball or score all the goals—you need to show them you're a team player, and that you have skills that will make you an asset on the team.

Remember: Not everyone who tries out will be selected. If you're not chosen for a team one year, keep practicing and come back the next year.

Coach Mike says: "Don't be heartbroken if you don't make a team. A lot of great players get cut from teams and develop their skills later. Believe in yourself and try out next year—or perhaps try out for another club's select program. The key is to keep playing and improving your skills—and have fun with the game!"

LEADERSHIP
OPPORTUNITIES

T HERE ARE MANY ways to be a team leader in soccer. The most obvious leadership oppor- tunity, of course, is to be selected as the team captain. But if you're not chosen as captain, there are plenty of other ways to step up and be an important leader on your team.

- Are you especially good at a specific skill—and do you offer to help your teammates figure out how to improve at it, too?
- Do you stay calm and collected during a tense match when it seems like everyone else is turning into a hothead?

- Do you always give it your all at practice, demonstrating the importance of hard work?
- Can everyone hear you cheer- ing on your teammates from the sidelines, inspiring every- one to stay positive (even when you're down 5–1)?

- Many opportunities will arise for you to be a leader on your team. The only way to be suc- cessful is to work together as a team—and everyone plays a different role on the team at different times. What's your starring role?

Coach Mike says: "I believe in the power of positive energy. If you are encouraging and optimis- tic, your teammates will follow your lead and it may inspire them to be more positive, too. Great attitudes are contagious and a huge asset on the field . . . especially when you're facing adversity and difficult situations. Be a leader!"

TOP SOCCER TOURNAMENTS

ONE OF THE great perks of being on a competitive team is the opportunity to participate in tournaments around the country (some teams even travel around the world!). There are incredible tournaments that take place all over—there may even be a famous tournament that takes place in or near your hometown. Below are just a few of the largest and most unique tournaments that soccer-crazy girls everywhere might get to compete in someday:

SCHWAN'S USA CUP

One of the largest tournaments in the country has been held every July in Minneapolis, Minnesota, for more than twenty-five years. The Schwan's USA Cup—with more than 1,000 participating teams—is the largest international youth soccer tournament in the Western Hemisphere.

MSC KICKOFF CLASSIC

One of the top-ranked soccer tournaments in the northeast United States is also the only major soccer tournament that takes place entirely in New York City! More than 500 teams from across the country get to go to New York and play soccer in the heart of the Big Apple.

WAGS TOURNAMENT

For almost forty years, the WAGS Tournament—in Washington, DC—has been the place for nationally ranked teams to showcase their skills every October.

THE DALLAS CUP

This tournament, which is held in Texas, brings together some of the top youth soccer clubs from around the world. Forty percent of the 180 participating teams come from outside the United States, another forty percent come from across the US, and twenty percent of the teams are from the Dallas area. This tournament draws in a lot of college coaches and pro scouts from all over the world, so it's a great place for future soccer stars to get noticed.

GOLDEN GOAL TOURNAMENT PARK

One of the most unique tournament facilities is the Golden Goal Tournament Park in New York's Adirondack Mountains. The organizers of Golden Goal strive to provide an environment that almost feels like a mini–Olympic Village. The park has weekly tournaments, and visiting teams stay with each other in Athlete Village. Players are able to bond with their own teammates, and also get to know players from other teams.

GETTING READY FOR THE GAME

PREGAME
RITUALS

MANY ATHLETES have pregame rituals—from listening to special music or watching playback from their last game, to eating a certain meal or rubbing a lucky charm. But some athletes have pretty crazy pregame rituals that take superstition to a whole new level.

A Canadian hockey player, Bruce Gardiner, had a tradition of dunking his stick in the toilet before every game. The night before basketball games, NBA player Jason Terry sleeps in his opponent's shorts—somehow, he has a pair of shorts from every other basketball team! Former NFL linebacker Brian Urlacher would eat exactly two chocolate chip cookies before every game.

What about soccer? Cristiano Ronaldo gets a haircut before every game. Legendary player George Best ate a chocolate bar before all his matches. And in the 1998 World Cup, French soccer player Laurent Blanc would plant a big kiss right on the top of the goalkeeper's bald head in every game. The lucky kisses worked—France beat Brazil to take home the World Cup!

The legendary University of North Carolina at Chapel Hill (UNC) women's team—which has won twenty-one national championships—has this ritual: Each team member puts a white piece of tape around her pinkie finger before games to symbolize their togetherness. Other women's soccer teams all sing or jam to a certain song during their warm-up or wear the same color headband to show their team spirit and solidarity.

Really get to know and establish relationships with your teammates, because they are your new family and they will be the ones there for you when anything goes wrong. —Alex Morgan

PUMP IT UP!

MANY SOCCER-CRAZY GIRLS—and other athletes—have a special song or playlist they like to listen to before a big game to get them pumped up and in the zone. Some like to listen to inspirational songs to get them mentally prepared, while others listen to fast songs to give them a burst of energy. Many athletes even listen to one song over and over again before they hit the field or pool or track. (US soccer star Alex Morgan loves to listen to "The Show Goes On" by Lupe fiasco before she hits the field.)

Everyone's playlist is unique, and if you're the kind of person who is moved by music, you should work on a special pregame playlist of your own. Of course, any song will do if it puts you in the right mood, but this is a list of some of the popular songs other athletes like to listen to—try a few and see how they make you feel.

- "We Will Rock You": Queen
- "Skyscraper": Demi Lovato
- "Crazy Train": Ozzy Osbourne
- "Back in Black": AC/DC
- "Express Yourself": Madonna
- "Eye of the Tiger": Survivor
- "More": Usher
- "Enter Sandman": Metallica
- "Fireworks": Katy Perry
- "Let's Get It Started": Black Eyed Peas

- "Fighter": Christina Aguilera
- "Stronger": Kanye West
- "Diva": Beyoncé
- "Gimme Three Steps": Lynyrd Skynyrd
- "Hero": Mariah Carey
- "Oh!": Union Turnpike
- "Right Now": Van Halen
- "Roar": Katy Perry
- "Go Getta": Lil Wayne
- "I Will Survive": Gloria Gaynor
- "Jump Around": House of Pain

- "Born to Win": Papoose
- "Welcome to the Jungle": Guns N Roses
- "Stronger (What Doesn't Kill You)": Kelly Clarkson
- "Heart of a Champion": Nelly
- "We Are One": 12 Stones
- "Pretender": Foo Fighters
- "The Final Countdown": Europe

SOCCER GEAR

L UCKILY, YOU DON'T need a lot of special gear to play soccer. In fact, you could play with nothing more than a ball, something to mark goals, and a friend or two—and that's exactly how many people around the world play every day. But if you're in any kind of organized league, there are a few basic things you will probably need.

- water bottle (Fig. A): Staying hydrated during practice and games will help keep your energy up
- shin guards (Fig. B): These are very important—and required by most leagues—for protecting your legs.

- cleats (Fig. C)
- soccer ball (Fig. D)
- soccer shorts
- soccer socks (Fig. E) (it's a good idea to have two pairs, in case one is in the wash or gets wet during the game)
- sports bra (Fig. F)

- headband or binders
- if you're a full-time goalkeeper, you'll also need a goalkeeper's jersey and gloves
- other things to include in your bag include athletic tape, sunscreen, bug spray, and a snack

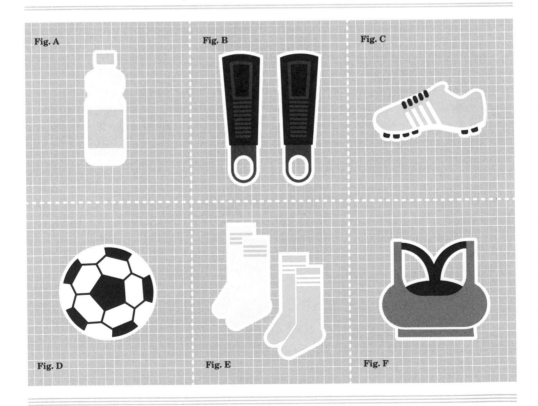

Fig. A Fig. B Fig. C

Fig. D Fig. E Fig. F

CLEATS OR BOOTS?

ALMOST EVERYONE WHO lives in the United States calls soccer shoes *cleats*. But just about everywhere else, *cleats* are called *boots*. Same shoe, different name.

CARE FOR YOUR CLEATS

WHEN YOU GET home from a game, it's tempting to throw your bag of gear on the floor so it's all packed for your next practice. But don't leave your cleats stuffed in your bag. Take a few minutes to pull them out, knock off the mud that's caked on the bottom, and wipe the leather with a damp cloth to get rid of any dirt. If your cleats are wet, stuff them with newspaper to absorb the moisture. If you take good care of them, they'll feel better and last longer.

S ★ O ★ C ★ C ★ E ★ R

SOME SOCCER PLAYERS are well-known for their amazing skills on the field . . . while others are even more famous for their wild personalities or crazy fashion sense. Since every player has to wear the same uniform on the field, one of the easiest ways a player can express his or her individuality during a game is with their hair—and some male soccer players have definitely put a lot of time and effort (and hair dye) into expressing themselves! A few of the soccer players with the most memorable hair

DJIBRIL CISSÉ: Cissé is a French player who seems to change his hair color and style with his moods. He uses different colors, shaving patterns, and facial hair to create a signature look that always makes him very recognizable both on and off the field.

CARLOS VALDERRAMA: As the captain of the Colombian team during three different World Cups, Valderrama was an exceptional player. But he got even more attention for his wild mop of blond curls and signature mustache.

in the net, but he was just as recognized for his long, shiny black curls.

for his play, but also because of his distinctive bleached-blond dreadlocks.

RENÉ HIGUITA: Higuita was a goalkeeper for the Columbian team. Nicknamed El Loco, he often left the penalty area to dribble the ball up the field to score goals himself! He was well-known for his impressive acrobatic skills

RIGOBERT SONG: Song has played for Cameroon in four World Cups—his first was in 1994 when he was just 17 years old. His fourth showing for the African nation was in the 2010 World Cup. Song always stood out on the field

ALEXI LALAS: Lalas was on the US National Team from 1991–1998, playing as a defender on the 1994 American World Cup team. Lalas's bushy reddish hair and beard made him instantly recognizable to fans everywhere.

(HAIR) STYLE

DAVID JAMES: James, an English goalkeeper, has tried just about everything when it comes to his hair: bleaching, dyeing, shaving, curling, dreadlocked, braided, long, short—and for the 2010 World Cup he grew his hair into a halo shape.

ABEL XAVIER: Xavier is a retired Portuguese player who tried out many different hairstyles during his career, some of which were pretty crazy-looking: a tidy blond bouffant, a braided mohawk, and a fuzzy blond-hair-and beard combo that looked a lot like a lion's mane.

Most professional female soccer players tend to keep their look a little more conservative, opting to focus on their skills on the field rather than their image. The most popular styles for women's soccer players include tidy braids, short cuts, or a simple ponytail and sweatband that keeps hair out of their eyes. What's your personal style?

STRETCH

DID YOU KNOW that during a professional soccer game, players run an average of six to seven miles? You might not be running that much during one of your matches, but you are going to be running a lot. So it's important to warm up your muscles before the game, and drink plenty of water during the game.

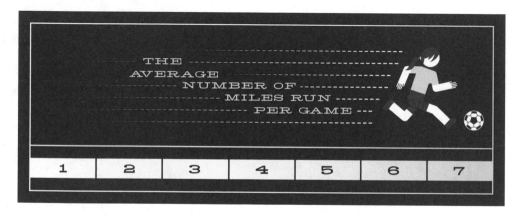

THE AVERAGE NUMBER OF MILES RUN PER GAME

| 1 | 2 | 3 | 4 | 5 | 6 | 7 |

STATIC STRETCHING VS. DYNAMIC STRETCHING

IN YEARS PAST, coaches and trainers have focused on **static stretching**—a player holds a series of stretches that each focus on one muscle group—before games and practice. People believed that static stretching could help protect play-ers from injury and would improve performance.

But in recent years, most professional soccer players have switched over to doing dynamic stretching before their games, rather than stat-ic stretching. Recent research has shown that static stretch-ing can cause muscle heavi-ness and fatigue, which is a problem in sports like soccer. **Dynamic stretching** rou-tines focus on warming up the body by doing things that get blood pumping by mimicking movements your body will make during the game.

HYDRATE,

HYDRATE!

MAKE SURE YOU don't wait until you're thirsty to get a drink of water during practice or a game. Drinking plenty of water is important at all times when you're playing, but it's essential on hot summer days. By the time you *feel* thirsty, you're probably already dehydrated—so keep that water bottle ready, and fuel your body with plenty of fluids!

SLEEP TIGHT

Your gear's packed, you're stretched and warmed up, you've had plenty of water . . . but is your body rested and ready to power you through practice or a game? One of the most important elements of becoming a world-class athlete is getting enough sleep. (Also important: Eating like a champion! See page 67 for more tips on how to keep your body working right for you.)

Your physical training on the field is essential, of course, but equally important is rest. Plenty of sleep is necessary for mental sharpness, but it's also a critical part of your muscle recovery. During rest, your body has a chance to repair and grow stronger. If you train hard but don't get enough sleep, you're not letting your body rebuild and recover—which can lead to injuries, sluggishness and decreased energy, slow reflexes, a higher likelihood of getting sick, and muscle loss. Training is important, but without enough sleep and the right kinds of foods, you could be doing more harm than good.

Try to get at least eight to ten hours of solid sleep a night, and you'll be ready to go all day long!

Coach Mike says: "Drinking too much water *right* before a game or practice can sometimes cause problems (such as needing to use the restroom mid-game, or getting a side ache). It's important to drink a lot of water in the hours before the game, to make sure you go into your practice or game well hydrated!"

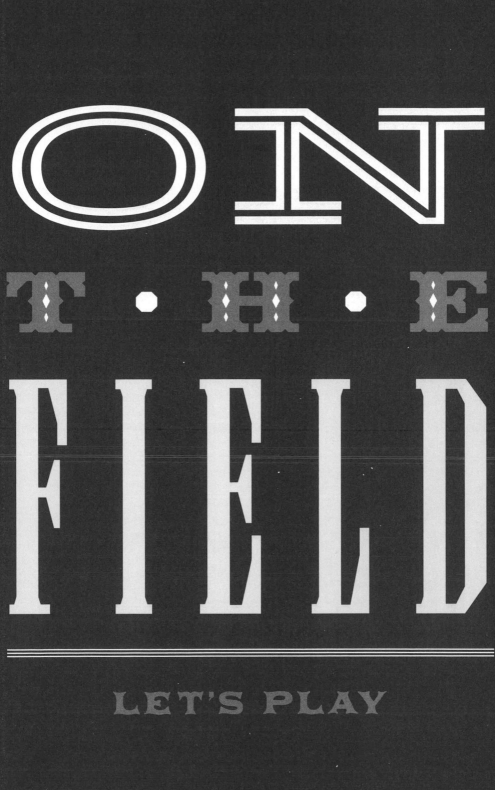

ON
T·H·E
FIELD

LET'S PLAY

I N MOST OTHER countries around the world, a soccer field is called a pitch. But no matter what it's called, a standard, official soccer field is usually laid out exactly the same. The outside of the field is made up of *touchlines* (which are also called *sidelines*) and *goal lines* (or *end lines*) at each end of the field. There is a striped line across the middle of the field (center line), with a circle marking the exact center (center circle).

Surrounding each goal is the *goal area*, which extends six yards out from the goal line. Beyond the *goal area* is the *penalty area*, which is eighteen yards out from the goal line. The goalkeeper is only allowed to touch the ball with her hands when she is inside the penalty area. Beyond that area, she can only kick it with her feet, like the rest of the players on the field.

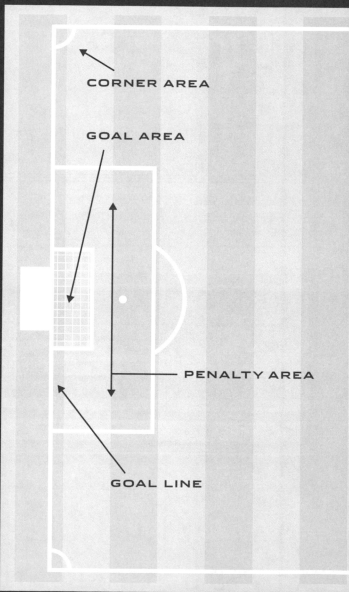

CORNER AREA

GOAL AREA

PENALTY AREA

GOAL LINE

FIELD

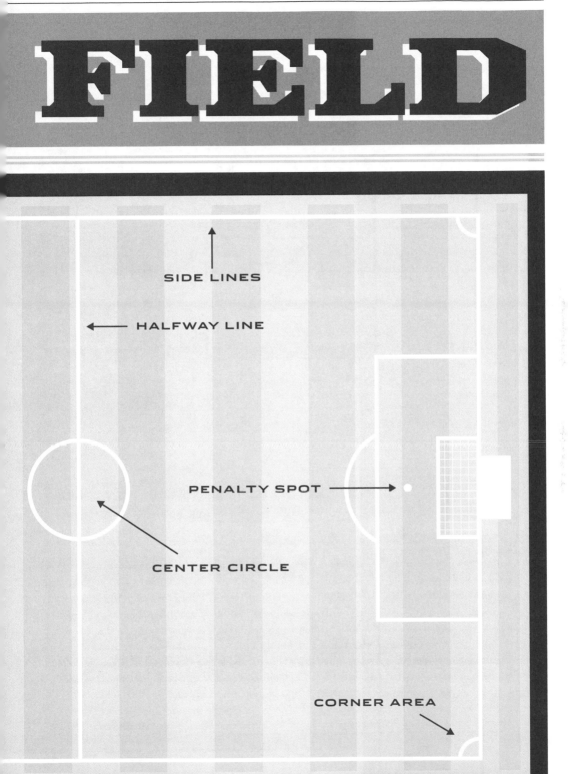

SIDE LINES

HALFWAY LINE

PENALTY SPOT

CENTER CIRCLE

CORNER AREA

· ALL ABOUT · THE BALL

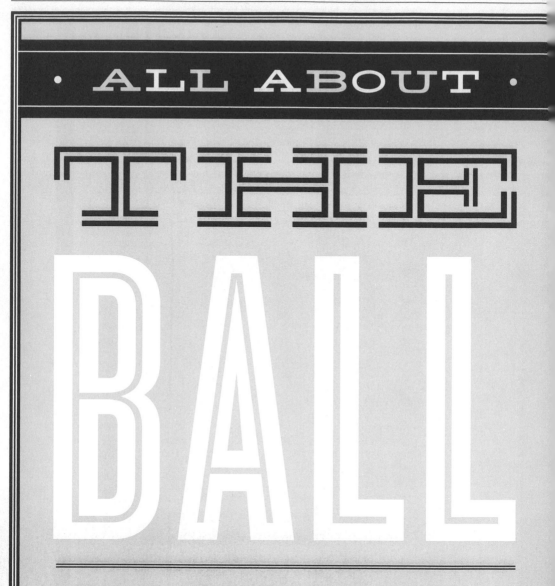

MOST MODERN SOCCER balls are stitched from 32 panels of waterproofed leather or plastic. Soccer balls come in three sizes that are authorized for match play.

SIZE 3: For children under the age of 8. Size 3 balls have a circumference of 23–24 inches and weigh 11–12 ounces.
SIZE 4: For players between ages 8 and 12. Size 4 balls have a circumference of 25–26 inches and weigh 12–13 ounces.

SIZE 5: These are the standard match ball for everyone 12 years and older. Size 5 balls have a circumference of 27–28 inches and weigh 14–16 ounces.

Of course, any ball—or any roundish object—will do if you're just playing for fun!

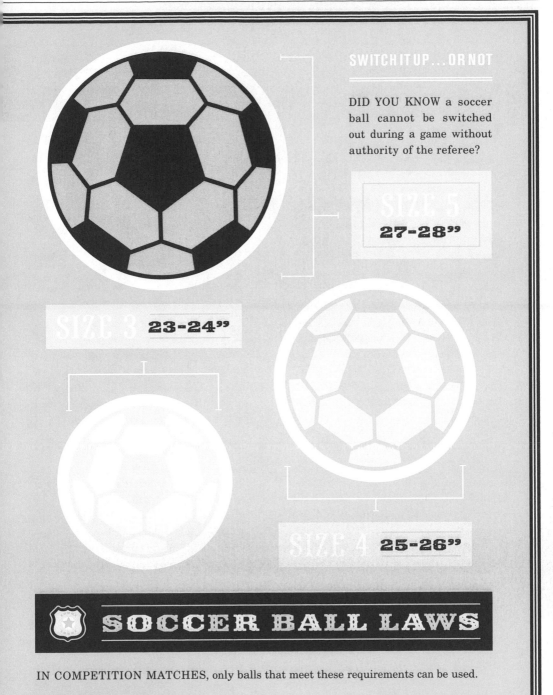

SWITCH IT UP...OR NOT

DID YOU KNOW a soccer ball cannot be switched out during a game without authority of the referee?

SIZE 5
27-28"

SIZE 3 23-24"

SIZE 4 25-26"

SOCCER BALL LAWS

IN COMPETITION MATCHES, only balls that meet these requirements can be used.

- spherical
- made of leather or other suitable material (for high school games it must also be weather-resistant)
- no more than 28 inches and not less than 27 inches in circumference
- between 14 and 16 ounces in weight at the start of the match

HOW TO

FORMATIONS & STRATEGIES

STRATEGY IS AN important part of a soccer game—and it's an important element for you to become more familiar with as you advance in your soccer career. Coaches think a lot about how to organize their players on the field, and will often use different *formations*—also called *systems*—depending on the players on the field, and the strengths of the opposing team.

If your team is full of strong midfielders, your coach will probably organize the team differently than she would if you had a lot of aggressive forwards or solid defenders. And if you happen to be playing a team full of powerful forwards, your coach will take that into consideration when organizing your defensive line. In leagues with younger players, formations and strategy aren't as important, but as you get into more competitive leagues, the way your team is organized on the field becomes a crucial consideration.

There are dozens of different ways to organize players on the field, and your coach is the best person to figure out what will work best at each game. Oftentimes, a coach will switch up strategy mid-game based on how things are progressing. If your team has a solid lead and wants to protect it, your coach may decide to employ a defensive formation or system—asking a forward player to drop back to midfield. But if you're behind, a coach may utilize a more aggressive attacking formation—sacrificing a defender to strengthen the attacking line.

Some of the most popular and common formations are outlined here. But there are dozens more to choose from, so always be ready to go with the flow and trust your coach's decision.

In each of these scenarios, the defensive players are listed first and then the numbers move up the field accordingly. So if a formation is listed as 1-4-4-2, that means one goalkeeper, four defenders, four midfielders, and two forwards.

THESE ARE JUST a few of the formations available for coaches to choose from, but there are many more variations. Some will work better at some times and with certain teams, while others might work better under different circumstances. It's important for a coach to consider the strengths of your team, as well as the strengths of your opponent, and then help set you up for the best chance of success. Trust in your coach to know what's best for your team.

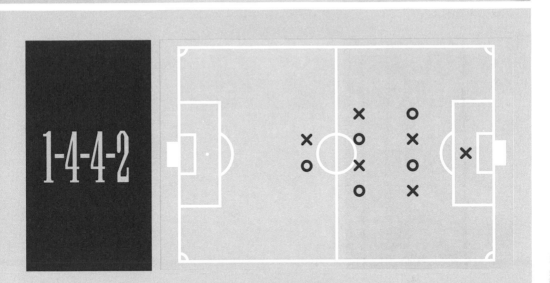

F OR MANY YEARS, this was the most common soccer formation. With a 1-4-4-2 (which is sometimes written as 4-4-2. The goalkeeper is obvious!) formation, the team relies on the midfielders to support both the defensive line and the forwards. But because there are four defenders, midfielders often need to move into an attacking role.

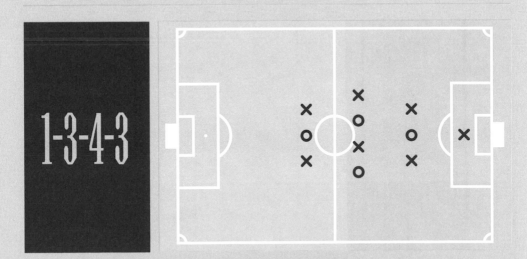

T HE MIDFIELDERS MUST be even more versatile in this system—splitting their time between attacking and defending. This can be a risky formation because the team sacrifices a defender to add a forward. However, it is typically an aggressive formation that encourages more attacking play.

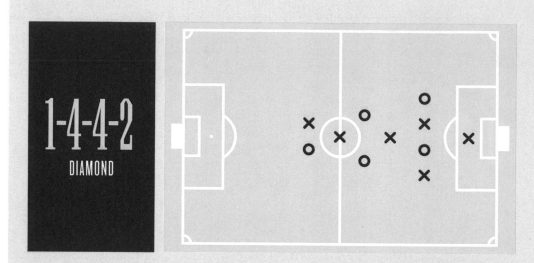

T HIS FORMATION IS sometimes described as 1-4-1-2-1-2, because the midfielders are staggered from back to front on the field. Instead of playing a solid line across, one defender is responsible for hanging back, and another is placed right behind the forwards so the midfield looks like a diamond.

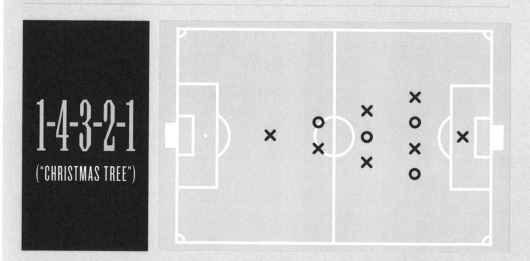

I N THIS FORMATION, two forwards are positioned slightly behind the other. One player is way up front to be a true attacker.

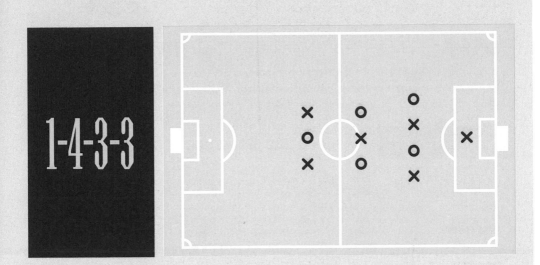

IN THIS FORMATION, coaches usually play with three center-midfielders and have their forwards and outside defenders defend and attack the sides of the field. Additionally, a coach will sometimes ask two of the forwards to drop back a bit to help the midfield, making it look more like a 1-4-5-1 formation.

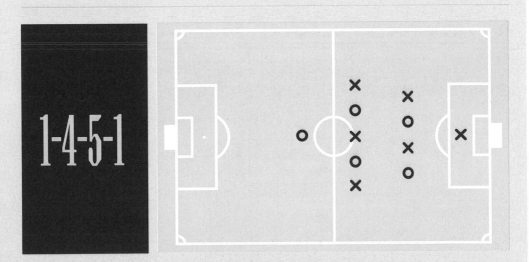

MANY PROFESSIONAL COACHES use this formation to keep their goal well defended, but the lone forward can get very tired up front alone.

FIELD TALK

COMMUNICATION IS KEY in soccer—after all, it's a team sport. So how do you best communicate with your teammates on the field? Here are some of the most frequently used phrases players or coaches will say during a game:

PHRASE	• • • MEANING • • •
MOVE UP/PUSH UP	Move up the field. (When defense moves up, it can create an offsides trap.)
I'M OPEN	I'm here to help—pass to me.
MAN ON	Someone's coming up behind you to try to steal the ball.
NO ONE	No one's behind you—go for it.
TIME	No one's coming—you have time with the ball, no pressure.
PRESSURE	Pressure the other players to try to steal the ball away or slow down the other team.
GET BACK	Drop back to defend the goalkeeper.
STAY ON SIDES	Look out—you're at risk of an offsides trap or call.
SUPPORT	You have a teammate behind you if you need to pass the ball backward.
DROP	I'm behind you and open for a pass.
SQUARE	I'm next to you and open—pass it.
THROUGH	Pass the ball through the opposing team to one of your forward-moving teammates.
SHOOT	Go for the goal!
TAKE HER ON	Try to get behind the opponent in front of you off the dribble.

DEFENSIVE STRATEGIES

THERE ARE TWO basic strategies a soccer coach will use to defend against the opposing team: man-on-man defense and zone defense.

MAN-ON-MAN: Each player guards against a specific player on the opposite team. With this defense, the best defenders can be pitted against the best offensive players on the other team. But even if you're using a man-on-man defense, it's important to step away from your mark if one of your teammates needs some help.

ZONE: When a coach uses zone defense, each defender guards a specific area of the field rather than a specific player. This defensive strategy requires great communication in the defensive line to make sure the field is well covered at all times.

FOULS ARE CALLED for many different reasons in soccer. If a player intentionally touches the ball with her hands or trips, pushes, or holds another player, a direct free kick or penalty kick is awarded to the player who was fouled. Other types of fouls—such as offside offenses or breaking minor technical rules—result in an indirect free kick.

For more severe (or repeated) fouls or extremely unsportsmanlike behavior, the referee may give a player a yellow or red card. A yellow card is considered a caution or warning. A red card is for the most serious offenses, and it results in an immediate dismissal from the game. Some of the reasons a referee might give a player a red card include

- using bad language or rude gestures
- violence toward another player—hitting, punching, kicking, etc.
- spitting at another player
- reckless or dangerous behavior that puts another player at risk
- blocking a possible goal-scoring shot by using hands or an intentional foul (like tripping someone on a breakaway)
- also, if a player gets a second yellow card in the same game, the two together become a red card and the player is ejected from the game

If a player is kicked off the field, the team cannot put a substitute on the field in their place. They must play with one less player for the rest of the game. In many leagues, a player who receives a red card in one game must also sit out at least one more game. So play fair out there!

A REFEREE'S
UNIFORM

I N AMERICAN SOCCER, referees' uniforms do not always look the same. While the official uniform is a yellow shirt, the United States Soccer Federation (USSF) has switched up things a few times over the past twenty years; sometimes you'll see refs wearing blue, black, red, or green shirts, in addition to yellow. Most of the time, referees' shirts will also have a pinstripe pattern. Many referees also sport a patch over their chest pocket—this patch means that the ref passed a test and is certified by the USSF.

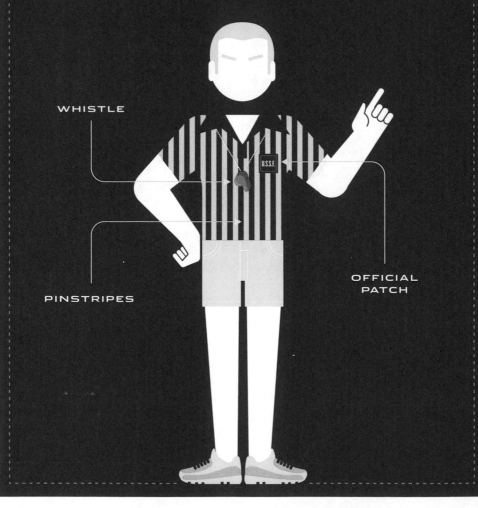

WHISTLE

U.S.S.F.

OFFICIAL
PATCH

PINSTRIPES

SHOOT-OUT!

IN LEAGUE COMPETITIONS, soccer games can end in a tie. But in tournaments, where a winner must be determined, the show must go on. And sometimes on and on and on.

A game that is tied at the end of regulation time—usually two forty-five-minute periods, plus a bit of injury time that is determined by the referee—may go into extra time. Extra time usually consists of two additional fifteen-minute periods. Goals that are scored during extra time count toward the final score of the game.

If the game is still tied after extra time, some competitions will then go to penalty shootouts. Penalty shoot-outs are officially called *kicks from the penalty mark* (twelve yards out from the goal line). Any goals scored during penalty shoot-outs do not count toward the final score of the game. Rather, they're just used to determine the winner of the match.

The opposing teams take turns kicking from the penalty mark until each team has taken five kicks (or until one team has scored more shots than the other could reach with its remaining turns). If the teams are still tied after the first five kicks, then the penalty kicks move into sudden-death elimination until one team emerges as the winner.

A few important rules for penalty kicks:

Only players who were on the field at the end of play are allowed to participate in the shoot-out—once a player leaves the game, she's out for good.

Teams can replace the goalkeeper if he or she is injured during the shoot-out—but only if the team hasn't already used up the maximum number of substitutes (three) for the game.

If a goalkeeper is sent out of the game during the shoot-out (for misconduct or otherwise), another player who was on the field at the end of the game must fill in.

No player can take a second kick from the penalty mark until all other eligible players have taken a turn—including the goalkeeper.

ONCE A SOCCER game starts, a ball is considered *in play* at all times, except when it leaves the field or the referee stops play. Once a ball is *out of play*, the ball can only be put back *in play* in one of these eight ways:

- **KICKOFF:** There is a kickoff after each goal, or to begin each period.

- **THROW-IN:** When the ball is kicked out of bounds, the team that *did not* touch it last gets a throw-in.

- **GOAL KICK:** If the ball crosses the goal line—without a goal—after being last touched by a player from the *attacking* team, then a goal kick is awarded to the *defending* team.

- **CORNER KICK:** If the ball crosses the goal line—without a goal—after being last touched by a player from the *defending* team, then a corner kick is awarded to the *attacking* team.

- **INDIRECT FREE KICK:** This is awarded to the opposing team after non-penalty fouls, certain technical infringements, or when the referee must stop play to caution or warn a player. In an indirect free kick, the kicker may not score a goal directly—the ball must first touch another player.

- **DIRECT FREE KICK:** These are awarded to a fouled team after certain fouls. A goal may be scored by the player who takes a direct free kick, even if the ball doesn't touch another player before going into the net.

- **PENALTY KICK:** Penalty kicks are awarded under the same circumstances as a direct free kick: when a foul is committed by a player within their opponent's penalty area.

- **DROPPED BALL:** The referee will signal for a dropped ball after play is stopped for any other reason, such as serious injury, interference by a fan or other non-player (like a dog or paper airplane on the field), or if a ball becomes defective.

WHAT YOUR POSITION SAYS ABOUT YOU

SOMETIMES, A PLAYER'S position on the field matches up really well with her personality *off* the field. But other times, the soccer field is the perfect place to discover a secret side of yourself that you never knew you had. Does your favorite position match up with the kind of person you are?

FORWARD: During a game and at practice, forwards need to be aggressive, confident, super-competitive, clever and quick thinkers, and fast. Many forwards are risk takers, and also tend to love the spotlight, since their job is to score and revel in the glory. Does that sound like you?

MIDFIELDER: Midfielders do more running than any other players on the field, so it's essential that they have a lot of endurance and speed. Because they are expected to help out all over the field, they also need to be obser-vant, quick thinking, excellent playmakers, and to have great passing skills. Midfielders need to be very smart and conscientious because they need to know when to attack and when to defend.

DEFENDER: Defensive players tend to be less moti-vated by fame and glory, since they score far fewer goals than their forward and midfield teammates. They are usual-ly great team players, stay calm under pressure, and are strong, confident, and consistent—a lot of the same qualities as a great friend!

GOALKEEPER: Goalkeep-ers need to have a positive attitude, thick skin, and be able to handle constant pres-sure—because oftentimes the outcome of the game (and the blame for a loss) falls on their shoulders. Also, with a ball sailing straight at them throughout the game, it's essential that goalkeepers be fearless and quick thinking. They have to react in an instant. Do you have the guts and confidence it takes to stand in front of the net?

PLAY SAFE

PREVENTING INJURIES ON THE PITCH

B EFORE EVERY PRACTICE AND game, it's important to get your body warmed up to help prevent injuries, muscle cramps, and after-game soreness. When you're a kid and your body is growing (believe me, you're growing a lot right now), your bones often grow faster than your muscles, which means you have even less natural flexibility. It's essential that you get your muscles warm before you jump into a game or scrimmage.

If you don't participate in sports during the off-season, it's also important to get yourself in shape before the soccer season starts. If your body is ready for action, you're much less likely to get injured when you hit the field those first few weeks of practice. Sprains and strains are more likely to occur at the beginning of the season because your body needs time to get back into shape. If you do some good exercises to strengthen your hamstring muscles (they run along the backs of your thighs) and quadriceps (the muscles on the front and insides of your thighs), it will really help you be more agile from day one. Also, if you start walking, running, or biking a bit before the season (or, even better, if you stay in shape all year!), it will help your body get fit again.

WARM-UP EXERCISES

YOUR COACH PROBABLY has a specific pregame warm-up routine that your team performs. While you are waiting for your team warm-up to start, it's a good idea to do some juggling or passing with a teammate or two. If you're just getting together with some friends to play for fun and want to run your own warm-up, here are some ideas:

1. Run back and forth across (or around) the field, or do some jumping jacks. Shake it up a little by doing zigzag running, backward jogging, and then some easy forward running. The important thing is to warm up your muscles, paying close attention to getting blood moving to your calves, quads, hamstrings, inner thighs, and your hips. Your coach, parents, or gym teachers probably have some good suggestions for dynamic pregame stretching if you need some ideas of how to warm up each of these muscle groups.

2. Now it's time to really get your heart pumping. Do some walking lunges, jump in place, power through some sprints, and get your body moving.

3. Before you play, take some time to do a few agility drills to make sure your knees and ankles are ready. Dribble the ball through cones, run diagonally across the field, play tag—anything that gets you moving in different directions and dodging around obstacles.

4. After you've finished playing, take a few minutes to do some static stretching and walk around to cool down. Also, drink plenty of water. All of these things will help prevent soreness and injury.

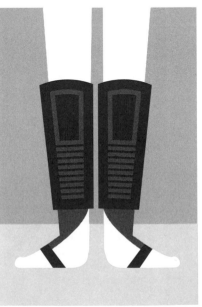

SHIN GUARDS

YOUR SHINS ARE in the middle of the action during a game, so it's essential that you protect them from impact. Always wear shin guards!

OUCH!
SOCCER INJURIES

THERE ARE SOME common—and not-so-common—injuries that you might experience during your career as a soccer player. These injuries range in seriousness from uncomfortable to season-ending, but the most important thing to remember is that no game is worth risking long-term pain or problems. Sometimes, small things can lead to big things (or re-injury), so make sure you always get someone—a parent, your coach, or a doctor—to check you out when something hurts to make sure you're not at risk of injuring yourself even more if you keep playing or don't get medical attention. Take care of yourself now so you can be there for your team through the rest of the season.

- **BLISTERS:** Blisters are fluid-filled bumps or bubbles on your skin that usually appear on hands or feet (sometimes they can be caused by cleats that don't fit quite right). Blisters are mostly just uncomfortable, but sometimes they can get infected, so it's important to take good care of them by keeping them clean and covered with a bandage while they're healing.

- **CUTS AND BRUISES:** Because there's so much running and jumping and diving for the ball in soccer, cuts and bruises are a regular (and expected) part of the game. Most cuts and bruises hurt at least a little bit, but they can usually be treated quickly on the field—to prevent scarring or infection—and get you back into the action.

- **CRAMPS:** Muscle cramps (sometimes called charley horses) occur when a muscle contracts and will not relax, causing sudden pain and tightness in a specific part of your body. The most common cramps for soccer players include side stitches and leg or foot cramps. Taking a short break to stretch, massage the muscle, and breathe deeply will often help cramps go away, but sometimes they require icing or heat. There are many different causes of muscle cramps—including tight muscles and dehydration—so always make sure you stretch before you play and remember to drink plenty of water. Eating bananas helps, too, as cramps can sometimes be caused by not enough potassium.

- **HEAT RASH:** Heat rash can be a problem for soccer players who are playing in hot and humid weather. Heat rash occurs when your sweat ducts get blocked, and it usually makes your skin red and itchy. Heat rash will usually get better on its own after you move to a cool and dry place.

- **INSECT STINGS:** Because soccer is often played outdoors, insects can be a real nuisance. For most people, insect stings are just annoying and painful. But for people who are allergic, insect stings can be serious—so it's important to be aware of the signs of an allergic reaction (such as mouth and throat itchiness, trouble breathing, and tightness of the chest), just in case.

- **SHIN SPLINTS:** Shin splints are a stress injury that cause a dull, aching pain in the front of the lower leg (your shin). Shin splints get worse over time and need to be treated with rest and medical attention.

- **SPRAINS:** Knee and ankle sprains are, unfortunately, fairly common in soccer because of all that running and contact with other players. Sprains occur when ligaments (the tough, elastic bands that connect your bones and hold your joints in place) get stretched or torn. If you've sprained something, it will probably swell up and be very uncomfortable. Sprains need to be treated with rest, ice, compression, and elevation (RICE)—so it's time to get off the field so you can heal!

- **STRAINS:** Muscle strains—also known as pulled muscles—happen when a muscle or tendon is stretched or torn. Warming up can help prevent muscle strain, as will good flexibility. The treatment for strains is similar to the treatment for sprains. If you do strain a muscle, it's important that you take care to make sure it's better before you play on.

- **BREAKS AND FRACTURES:** Broken bones are one of the more serious issues athletes have to deal with, since they require a player to take so much time to recover off the field. Luckily, they're rare, but fractures do sometimes happen on the soccer field. If you think you or a teammate or friend might have fractured a bone, make sure you get an adult's help right away.

- **HEAT ILLNESSES:** Heat stroke and heat exhaustion are both serious conditions that need to be treated immediately. It's easier to prevent heat illnesses than it is to treat them—so if you're playing on a hot day, wear light, loose clothing and sunscreen, and take care to stay hydrated. If you are playing in hot conditions and you feel the beginning of a headache or are starting to feel dizzy or nauseous, stop playing right away and look for a cool, shaded place to take a break and drink some water.

- **HEAD INJURIES:** Most people think of concussions when they think of head injuries, but mouth and eye injuries also sometimes occur on the soccer field. Most often, head injuries (including concussions) are the result of colliding with the goal post or another player. Head injuries can be very serious, so it's important to get immediate medical care.

HEADGEAR

BECAUSE SOCCER IS a contact sport, there is a risk of concussion and other head injuries during play. In recent years, headgear (such as header bands and headguards) has become more popular—and some teams and leagues are now requiring it—because it may help lower the risk of concussions. Soccer headgear may help spread the force of impact if you hit something (or someone) with your head. There's still a lot of research and development being done in this area, so talk to your coach, doctor, and parents about whether headgear might be a good addition to your gear list.

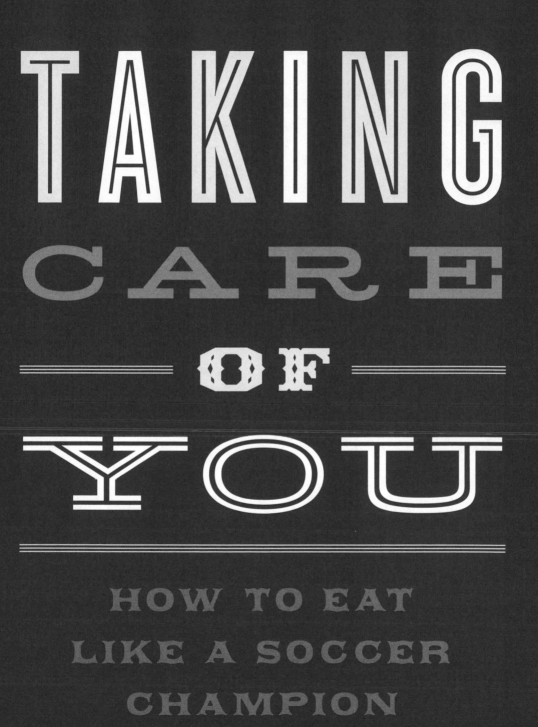

TAKING CARE OF YOU

HOW TO EAT LIKE A SOCCER CHAMPION

I T'S ESSENTIAL TO TAKE CARE OF your body, especially if you're an athlete. If you treat your body right—by eating enough of the right kinds of foods—it will be able to work better and harder during games and practices, and you'll have much more energy to showcase your skills on the field. Your doctor and parents are great people to talk to in more detail about healthy food choices, but we'll cover some of the basics here to get you heading down the right track and out onto the field with plenty of energy.

You probably already know that eating lots of fresh fruits and vegetables is great for your body. But what other foods will help you stay healthy, fast, and strong for soccer season? Are some snacks better than others? Want some ideas for great energy-boosting pregame meals and halftime snacks? Then read on!

PREGAME MEALS

I T'S VERY IMPORTANT to eat a great meal or snack before practice or a game. We've all had days when we haven't eaten enough good foods before hitting the park or the field. After playing on an empty or badly fed belly, you probably noticed yourself getting more tired and cranky than usual. Your muscles are like a machine, and they need the right kinds of fuel to keep you running and working properly.

What you put into your body definitely makes a difference in how you perform on the field. Some of the best things you can eat before you play soccer are grains (things like pasta or bread or crackers), because they're carbohydrates and they give your body energy. If you're going to be playing for more than an hour or so, you probably want to load up on some protein or low-fat fiber, too, to make that energy last longer. Both proteins and fibers take longer to digest, so they'll keep you moving a little longer than just carbohydrates can on their own.

Sometimes it's easiest to grab something unhealthy just to have *something* before you head out to the field. Soda, candy, and sugary snacks are often close and convenient on your way out the door—but they won't keep your body running well. They will give you some immediate energy, but you'll be running on empty after not too long. Instead, fill up on something with good carbohydrates and/or protein, such as:

- whole-grain bread, crackers, or cereal
- a bagel with peanut butter
- pretzels
- low-fat cheese or yogurt
- turkey, chicken, or tofu
- fresh fruit or vegetables
- fig bars or oatmeal cookies

Coach Mike says: "The great players enjoy treats now and then, but they always make sure it's part of an overall healthy diet. Talk to your parents about eating healthy, so your whole family can make great choices!"

WHAT ARE CARBOHYDRATES?

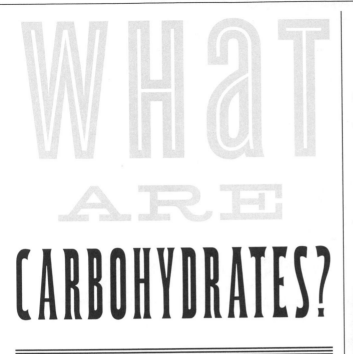

C ARBOHYDRATES (OR *CARBS*) are found in many kinds of food that help give athletes fuel that keeps them moving better and longer. There are two kinds of carbohydrates: simple and complex.

Simple carbohydrates—also called simple sugars, because your body digests them quickly to turn them into easy energy—are found in things like sugar, milk, and fruit. Some simple carbs are better for you than others. Plain white sugar and foods with sugar added—like candy, soda, and lollipops—will often give you a quick burst of energy, but they don't have any nutrients to fuel your body, and the energy you get from them will burn away after just a short time. But there are also some great sources of simple carbs. Milk is full of protein and calcium that will help your bones and muscles, and fruit is filled with healthy vitamins and fiber that help your body run more efficiently.

Complex carbohydrates—which take longer for your body to break down—are found in starches like bread, crackers, rice, pasta, and oatmeal, and also in many vegetables like carrots, corn, and potatoes. White—or *refined*—complex carbs are not nearly as good for you as whole-grain versions of the same food, because things like white bread and white pasta do not have as many great nutrients and fiber as whole-grain versions of these carbohydrates do. So when you're loading up on complex carbs, remember to choose whole-grain starches and veggies whenever you can to give your body a little extra *oomph* and energy that will last longer on the field.

WHAT IS FIBER?

Y OU'LL HEAR PEOPLE say that fiber is great for your body. But what is fiber, and what kinds of foods have it? fiber helps your digestive system work more efficiently and also helps you feel full longer.

Some great sources of fiber include

1 Fresh fruit

2 Vegetables

3 Whole-grain breads, cereals, crackers, and pasta

4 Beans and legumes (dried beans, split peas, and lentils)

5 Almonds

WHAT IS PROTEIN?

PROTEIN IS AN important nutrient that helps build your muscles and organs. It also helps repair cuts and tears, and aids your body in building up antibodies that fight diseases. It's good to eat foods high in protein after a game or workout.

Protein is found in many delicious foods, such as

- Meat (chicken, fish, turkey)
- Eggs
- Nuts and seeds
- (including peanut butter!)
- Dairy products (milk, yogurt, pudding, cheese)
- Beans (lentils, black beans, soybeans)
- Broccoli

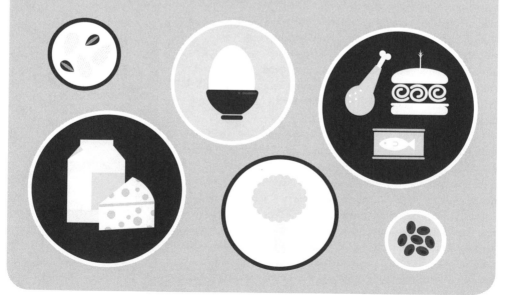

HALFTIME SNACKS

DURING HALFTIME, it's a good idea to refuel with something that makes sure your body will have enough energy for the second half of the game. The most important thing you can do at halftime is drink up. Your body needs water, so make sure you're drinking plenty of water or a sports drink (like Gatorade or Powerade) to stay hydrated while you're resting on the sidelines.

So what's the best snack to give you an energy boost during a long game or practice? Your body is working hard to keep you running—and not focusing on digesting food—so simple, quick snacks are best. Fruit is a great choice. Most fruit has a lot of water and important nutrients. There's a tradition of teams eating orange slices at halftime—orange slices are easy to eat, taste great, and have great body-boosting vitamin C. Bananas or grapes are also two quick and easy options.

Hard-boiled eggs are another fun idea for a portable snack. They come in their own packaging, and give your body a great burst of protein to keep up your energy in the second half. A whole-grain mini bagel or slice of bread with peanut or almond butter combines two good things: The bagel has carbohydrates to give you quick energy, while the nut butter has protein. Nuts or pretzels are another good choice.

The most important thing is that you find something that makes you feel great for the second half of the game. Some kids might find that fruit gives them a stomachache if they eat it during the game. Others might get a side ache or feel tired if they have anything other than a sports drink between halves. You have to figure out what works best for you—try different foods during practices to see what keeps you running most efficiently. Just remember to keep your body nourished and well fed every day to keep it in top working order.

AFTER-GAME FUEL

AFTER A GAME or a long practice, you'll probably be starving. Make sure you drink plenty of water to replace all the fluid you lost while you were playing (milk is another great drink option for after exercise). Then eat a healthy meal or snack to reward your body for a job well done. Of course, it's also important to celebrate a job well done—if your team goes out for pizza after a game, that's great, too! Some other ideas for good postgame snacks include

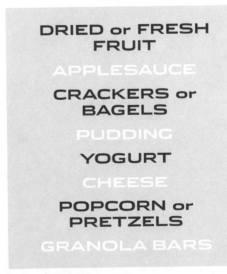

DRIED or FRESH FRUIT

APPLESAUCE

CRACKERS or BAGELS

PUDDING

YOGURT

CHEESE

POPCORN or PRETZELS

GRANOLA BARS

I WANT TO DO THAT!

SOCCER JOBS

I F YOU THINK YOU MIGHT WANT TO play soccer professionally someday, there are some important things you will need.

• **DEDICATION**: You must be committed, because the path to becoming a professional athlete takes a great deal of time, sacrifice, and effort.

• **THICK SKIN**: There will be rejection along the way—for every player—regardless of your skill level. You need to be able to take this rejection with grace and professionalism . . . and then get back up and keep trying.

• **DETERMINATION AND FOCUS**: You need to be willing to push yourself to the limit at every practice and game, focusing on mastering the fundamental elements of soccer.

• **TIME AND SACRIFICE**: You'll sometimes have to miss out on parties, school and family events, and other sports to give yourself completely to soccer.

• **EXPERIENCE**: Join a team and demonstrate your skills so you can continue to improve and get noticed. But also spend time watching other people play, trying to learn as much as you can from other players.

• **PATIENCE**: Every professional soccer player started out as a kid, just like you. Remember that the most important thing you can do as a young player is practice, practice, practice. And, of course, have fun while you're at it—don't worry about going pro for a while!

MONEY TALK$

S O HOW MUCH money does a professional soccer player make anyway? Honestly, not much. The very best players in the world make more than $10 million dollars a year (a few of the top male players make almost double that). But an average male player probably makes somewhere around $100,000 a year—and most female soccer players make much, much less than that. Many of the players in the MLS make less than $35,000 a year . . . about as much as a bricklayer, news reporter, or an elementary school teacher. But when you add in all the fun travel, screaming fans, and days spent doing what you love, it's a really great job.

$20 MILLION
The Very Best Male Players in the World

$10 MILLION
The Very Best Players in the World

$100,000
An Average Male Player

$35,000
Most Players in the MLS

MAJOR LEAGUE SOCCER
(MLS)

T HE MEN'S PROFESSIONAL soccer league in the United States is called Major League Soccer (MLS). The MLS was formed in 1996, and there are currently 14 teams in cities all around the country. Before MLS was formed, professional male soccer players played for the North American Soccer League (NASL), but the NASL folded in 1984. Between 1984 and 1996, there was no professional soccer league for men in the United States at all.

TOP
MEN'S
SOCCER CLUBS

MAJOR LEAGUE SOCCER (MLS) TEAMS

Eastern Conference:

- Chicago Fire
- Columbus Crew
- D.C. United
- Houston Dynamo
- Montreal Impact (Canada)
- New England Revolution
- New York Red Bulls
- Philadelphia Union
- Sporting Kansas City
- Toronto FC (Canada)

Western Conference:

- Chivas USA
- Colorado Rapids
- FC Dallas
- Los Angeles Galaxy
- Portland Timbers
- Real Salt Lake
- San Jose Earthquakes
- Seattle Sounders FC
- Vancouver Whitecaps FC (Canada)

Future Teams (begin play in 2015):

- New York City FC
- Orlando City SC

North American Soccer League (NASL):

- Atlanta Silverbacks
- Carolina RailHawks
- FC Edmonton (Canada)
- Fort Lauderdale Strikers
- Indy Eleven
- Minnesota United FC
- New York Cosmos
- Ottawa Fury FC
- San Antonio Scorpions
- Tampa Bay Rowdies

Future Teams:

- Jacksonville Armada FC
- Oklahoma City FC
- Virginia Cavalry FC

WOMEN'S NATIONAL SOCCER LEAGUES

WOMEN'S SOCCER IN the United States has gone through a lot of changes since 2001. Women's United Soccer Association (WUSA)—the original professional women's soccer league in the United States—was founded in February 2000, after the US Women's National Team took first place in the 1999 Women's World Cup. Because of the national team's success, people realized there might be interest in a professional women's league. There were eight teams in the league, and the first WUSA game took place in April 2001. Unfortunately, the league lost money and shut down in September 2003 after only three seasons of play.

When WUSA folded, the only other option for professional women's soccer players in the United States was in the Women's Premier Soccer League (WPSL). The WPSL is a national soccer league that oversees a mix of both professional and amateur teams. Each individual team in the league decides if they'll play as a pro or amateur team. Whether a team is pro or amateur is an important distinction for up-and-coming players, since anyone who wants to play for a college team must play in an amateur league—you are not allowed to play professionally while you're also a member of your university's team.

In 2009, six years after WUSA folded, the Women's Professional Soccer (WPS) league was formed as the next all-professional league in the United States. There were seven WPS teams for the first two seasons, but only six teams remained in 2011. The league canceled their season in January 2012, and then WPS closed down completely in May of that year.

A few months later, the WPSL formed Women's Premier Soccer League Elite (WPSL Elite), and three former WPS teams joined up with this league. But after just one season of WPSL Elite, yet *another* new top-level professional league was formed for women's soccer in spring 2013. The National Women's Soccer League (NWSL) kicked off its first season in April 2013 with eight teams, some of whom moved over from WPS and WPSL Elite.

Whew! That's a lot of different leagues in the past few years . . . can you keep them all straight? Ultimately, the names of the leagues really don't matter. The important thing is that we have a great place for women to play professional soccer in the United States. It's up to soccer-crazy girls everywhere to support all of the incredible teams and players so that professional women's soccer in America will be successful.

National Women's
Soccer League

BOSTON BREAKERS

CHICAGO RED STARS

FC KANSAS CITY

HOUSTON DASH

PORTLAND THORNS FC

SEATTLE REIGN FC

SKY BLUE FC

WASHINGTON SPIRIT

WESTERN NEW YORK FLASH

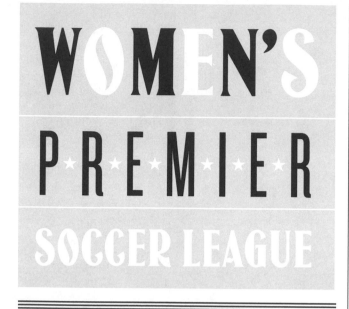

THE WPSL IS the largest women's soccer league in the world. Formed in 1998, the league's mission is to provide high-level soccer in communities throughout North America and Puerto Rico, and be a stepping stone for aspiring professional soccer players. Together with the W-League, WPSL is in the second tier of women's soccer in North America.

THE W-LEAGUE WAS the first women's soccer league in North America. In addition to giving elite amateur players the opportunity to compete alongside international and pro soccer stars, the W-League's amateur teams also allow college athletes to maintain their eligibility for university play.

There are WPSL and W-League teams throughout the United States and Canada—find the team nearest you and become a fan (if you're not already)!

CENTRAL CONFERENCE:

- K-W United FC
- Laval Comets
- London Gryphons
- Ottawa Fury
- Quebec Dynamo ARSQ
- Toronto Lady Lynx

NORTHEASTERN CONFERENCE:

- Fredericksburg Impact
- Long Island Rough Riders
- New Jersey Wildcats
- New York Magic
- North Jersey Valkyries
- Virginia Beach Piranhas
- Washington Spirit Reserves

SOUTHEASTERN CONFERENCE:

- Atlanta Silverbacks
- Carolina Elite Cobras
- Charlotte Lady Eagles
- Dayton Dutch Lions
- VSI Tampa Bay FC

WESTERN CONFERENCE:

- Bay Area Breeze
- Colorado Rush
- Colorado Storm
- LA Strikers
- Pali Blues
- Santa Clarita Blue Heat
- Seattle Sounders Women

WPSL TEAMS

PACIFIC CONFERENCE:

- California Storm
- North Bay FC Wave
- San Francisco Nighthawks
- West Coast Wildkatz
- Beach Futbol Club
- LA Premier FC
- San Diego WFC SeaLions

BIG SKY CONFERENCE:

- Phoenix Del Sol
- Real Salt Lake Women
- Tucson Soccer Academy
- FC Tulsa Spirit
- Fort Worth Panthers
- Houston Aces
- Houston South Select
- OCFCWP

NORTHWEST CONFERENCE:

- AC Seattle
- Eugene Metro Futbol Club
- Issaquah Soccer Club
- THUSC Diamonds
- Westside Timbers

SUNSHINE CONFERENCE:

- FC Surge
- Florida Sol FC
- Pinellas County United SC
- Team Boca Blast

SOUTHEAST CONFERENCE:

- Alabama FC
- Georgia Revolution
- Knoxville Lady Force
- Mississippi Fuego FC

MIDWEST CONFERENCE:

- Columbus Eagles
- Des Moines Menace
- FC Pride
- Fire & Ice FC
- Kansas City Shock
- Madison 56ers
- Minnesota TwinStars
- Ohio Galaxies

NORTHEAST CONFERENCE:

- Boston Aztec
- Boston Breakers College Academy
- CFC Passion
- New England Mutiny
- Seacoast United Mariners
- Seacoast United Phantoms
- Empire Revs WNY
- FC Westchester
- Syracuse Lady Knights
- Tri-City Celtics
- Yankee Lady FC
- BuxMont Torch FC
- FC Bucks
- FC LVU Lady Sonic
- Long Island Fury
- New York Athletic Club
- Jersey Blues FC
- ACF Torino USA (Maryland)
- ASA Chesapeake Charge
- Lions Swarm

SOCCER AT THE OLYMPICS: GOLD MEDAL WINNERS

WOMEN'S RESULTS:

- 1996: United States
- 2000: Norway
- 2004: United States
- 2008: United States
- 2012: United States

MEN'S RESULTS:

- 1900: Upton Park FC (England)
- 1904: Galt FC (Ontario)
- 1908: Great Britain
- 1912: Great Britain
- 1920: Belgium
- 1924: Uruguay
- 1928: Uruguay
- 1932: No Football Tournament
- 1936: Italy
- 1948: Sweden
- 1952: Hungary
- 1956: Soviet Union
- 1960: Yugoslavia
- 1964: Hungary
- 1968: Hungary
- 1972: Poland
- 1976: East Germany
- 1980: Czechoslovakia
- 1984: France
- 1988: Soviet Union
- 1992: Spain
- 1996: Nigeria
- 2000: Cameroon
- 2004: Argentina
- 2008: Argentina
- 2012: Mexico

US WOMEN'S NATIONAL TEAM

THE US WOMEN'S National team (sometimes referred to as USWNT or Team USA) is made up of the greatest female soccer players from across the United States. This team of elite soccer superstars represents the USA at the Olympics and the World Cup every four years. Team USA won the very first Women's World Cup in 1991. After that, Team USA also won four Olympic gold medals in women's soccer, and were the Women's World Cup Champions in 1999.

OLYMPIC DEVELOPMENT PROGRAM

THE US YOUTH Soccer Olympic Development Program (ODP) was formed in 1977 to identify the top soccer players in the United States. The ODP is responsible for finding, selecting, and developing the top players in each age group who will represent the United States in international competition. Nearly 100,000 players ages 13–18 from all over the United States take part in the ODP every year.

If you want to get involved in the ODP, it's important to contact your local US Youth Soccer State Association office. Every State Association holds open ODP tryouts every year in each of the five age groups. Players are evaluated in the four key elements of soccer: technical ability (technique), tactical (strategy), physical (fitness and athletic ability), and psychological (attitude). Once someone is selected for a state team, he or she can have the opportunity to move on to a higher level of play, such as Regional Teams and the National Camp.

HOW TO MAKE TEAM USA

SO HOW DOES the US Women's National Team coach find the very best players in the country to play on the team? Every year, the ODP program from each state sends a team of their best players to a Regional Camp. At this Regional Camp, a top team emerges with the best players in the whole region. Then National Camps and Interregional events help find the very top players in the whole country. The National Team Coach or a National Staff Coach attends these events to observe, train, and choose players for the national pool or the US National Team.

In 2009, however, the Elite Clubs National League (ECNL) was formed as an alternate way to be "discovered." Exceptional players can try out for ECNL teams (if you're lucky enough to have a team in your area—some states don't have a single ECNL team). If you make one of these elite teams, there's a lot of opportunity to get great exposure to important coaches and recruiters, and to participate in the highest level of competition and development in the United States.

OTHER SUPER SOCCER CAREERS

WHEN YOU IMAGINE what your life will be like, do you only see soccer, soccer, and more soccer in your future? The good news is, even if you don't end up playing professional soccer for a living (not many people do), there are plenty of other jobs that can keep you connected to your favorite sport. Here are a few job ideas for soccer-loving girls:

COACH: Many great coaches are former players who want to pass along their knowledge and passion to other players. Coaching is a great job for someone who absolutely loves soccer and wants an active job with a lot of important responsibility. Soccer coaches develop individual player's skills, and help lead their teams to victory. Professional coaches go through a lot of training to coach at colleges and schools, some competitive youth leagues, camps, and of course, the professional leagues. If you want to be a soccer coach, you need to be a great communicator, you have to know the ins and outs of soccer, and you have to be really passionate about the game and your players. As the coach, your whole team relies on you to keep things organized and rolling—if this sounds great, then coaching may be a good career for you.

Coach Mike says: "Coaching is very rewarding because the game can teach you about a lot more than just soccer!"

REFEREE: Professional referees go through extensive training to become experts in the rules of the game. US Soccer has more than 140,000 registered referees who work at all levels of the game, from youth soccer up to the professional soccer leagues. Like coaching, refereeing is a very active job, so if you like to run around a lot, love to follow and enforce rules (and don't mind people yelling at you from time to time), being a referee is another great soccer career.

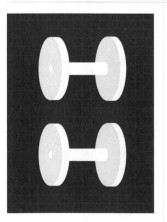

ATHLETIC TRAINER: An athletic trainer is a certified health-care professional who focuses on sports medicine. A trainer works with the coaching staff or at a clinic to help players prevent injury, diagnose problems, and rehabilitate players who are injured. Athletic trainers need to go through a lot of schooling to get certified to work as a trainer with a team and athletes. If you love learning about medicine and the human body, enjoy helping people get better, and are able to think on your feet, perhaps a career as an athletic trainer would be a good job option for you.

ASSOCIATION JOBS: There are many opportunities to get involved in soccer associations (such as American Youth Soccer Organization or FIFA) and professional or educational organizations. Some people run competitions, others organize clubs and camps, and many universities hire athletic directors for their athletic programs. Many people handle money and budgets, other people deal with marketing and advertising for events and teams, other people work on computer programming, and others help keep soccer organizations running smoothly from day to day. You certainly don't need to be a player or a coach to be involved in a soccer association.

STADIUM JOBS: If you work in a town that has a stadium or athletic field, there are probably some part-time or full-time jobs working at the stadium, selling merchandise or food, taking tickets, or cleaning. It's a great way to be a part of sporting events while getting paid.

MANUFACTURERS AND DISTRIBUTORS: If you know a lot about soccer and other sports equipment, you could get a job at a sporting goods store or work with a business that sells shoes, balls, shin guards, and more to teams and soccer programs. There are also jobs available working for sporting goods manufacturers, where you could help make sports equipment or sell and distribute sports equipment to stores.

THESE ARE JUST a few ideas for how you can get involved in a career that will keep you close to soccer every day of your life. But there are also a lot of excellent opportunities to stay involved with soccer in a nonprofessional way. You can always volunteer to help out as an assistant or junior coach for a neighborhood league—an opportunity that will immerse you in soccer in a very different capacity.

As an adult, you can play pickup soccer with friends or neighbors, or you can join rec teams. You can volunteer to help out as a coach, referee, or manager in a youth or adult recreational league, and you can share your knowledge and passion with high school or junior high school students as assistant coach or coach. If you love soccer, you'll always have a chance to participate in the game as much as you want!

ACCORDING TO FIFA, THERE ARE more than 265 million people in more than 200 countries who are actively involved in some form of organized soccer—making it the most popular game in the world. But there are many more people around the world who play soccer every day, just for fun.

FIFA

THE GOVERNING BODY of soccer is called **FIFA (Fédération Internationale de Football Association, or International Federation of Association Football)**. FIFA was founded in 1904 in Paris, and now its headquarters is in Zurich, Switzerland. There are more than 200 national association members of FIFA around the world. FIFA is in charge of the organization of all major international soccer tournaments—most notably the World Cup—and oversees everything that has to do with association football, futsal, and beach soccer in all countries around the world.

A GAME BY ANY OTHER NAME

ARE YOU SOCCER-CRAZY . . . or football-crazy? Outside North America, the game of *soccer* is called *football* (and the sport Americans call *football* is sometimes referred to as *gridiron* or *American football*). Calling the sport football makes a lot of sense, since the game we all love is played with your, uh, feet.

So why do North Americans have a different name for the game? The word soccer actually originated in England, where football is officially called *Association Football*. This was often shortened to *assoc* as a nickname (or *socca*). Since Americans already had a sport called football, the name *soccer* was adopted. Same game, different name.

MEMORABLE MOMENTS IN HISTORY

- **1904:** The Olympic Games (held in St. Louis, Missouri) included men's soccer as an Olympic sport for the first time. Club teams—playing under their national banners—represented the participating countries.

- **1930:** Thirteen countries (including the United States) participated in the first FIFA Men's World Cup.

- **1991:** The first FIFA Women's World Cup game was played in China. The US Women's National team won in the championship match against Norway.

- **1996:** The US Women's National Team won the first-ever gold medal in women's soccer at the Summer Olympics.

- **1999:** The United States's first women's professional league (WUSA) was formed, after the US Women's National Team beat China in a dramatic shootout to become FIFA Women's World Cup Champions once again.

T·H·E
OLYMPICS

M EN'S SOCCER HAS been played in every summer Olympics—except 1936—since 1900. But women's soccer has only been included in the Games since the 1996 Summer Olympics held in Atlanta, Georgia. The US Women's National team has won the gold medal four times—in 1996, 2004, 2008, and 2012—and the team went home with the silver medal in 2000, after losing to Norway in the gold medal match.

MEN'S FIFA WORLD CUP

T HE MOST POPULAR soccer tournament worldwide is the FIFA World Cup, which has been held every four years since 1930 (except in 1942 and 1946, when it was canceled because of World War II).

In the Men's World Cup, 32 teams qualify to compete for the title during the World Cup finals. The month-long World Cup finals take place at multiple venues throughout the host country. The famous tournament consists of a group stage, followed by a knockout stage—eventually leading to the crowning of the champion.

Most people are familiar with the World Cup finals, but many don't realize there is a long and highly competitive World Cup qualification phase. The qualifications take place over several years leading up to the World Cup finals, where teams compete in a series of regional matches to determine the finalists. There are six FIFA continental zones (Africa, Asia, North and Central America and Caribbean, South America, Oceania, and Europe), and FIFA determines how many teams from each zone can participate the World Cup finals. The format of the qualification tournaments is different in each region. For the 2010 FIFA World Cup, 204 countries entered the regional qualification rounds, but only 32 rose to the top as finalists!

MEN'S FIFA WORLD CUP CHAMPIONS

- 1930: Uruguay
- 1934: Italy
- 1938: Italy
- 1950: Uruguay
- 1954: West Germany
- 1958: Brazil
- 1962: Brazil
- 1966: England
- 1970: Brazil
- 1974: West Germany
- 1978: Argentina
- 1982: Italy
- 1986: Argentina
- 1990: West Germany
- 1994: Brazil
- 1998: France
- 2002: Brazil
- 2006: Italy
- 2010: Spain

FUTURE WORLD CUP HOST COUNTRIES

- 2018: Russia (first-ever Eastern European host country)
- 2022: Qatar (first-ever Middle Eastern host country)

WOMEN'S FIFA WORLD CUP

THE FIRST FIFA Women's World Cup (originally called the Women's World Championship) was held in 1991 in China, 61 years after the men's first FIFA World Cup. The Women's World Cup finals consist of 16 qualifying teams, and games take place over approximately three weeks.

WOMEN'S WORLD CUP CHAMPIONS:

- 1991: United States
- 1995: Norway
- 1999: United States

- 2003: Germany
- 2007: Germany
- 2011: Japan

FUTURE WOMEN'S WORLD CUP HOST COUNTRIES

- 2015: Canada (in 2015, the tournament will expand from 16 to 24 teams)

WORLD CUP AWARDS

AT THE END of each World Cup tournament, several additional awards are presented to exceptional players and teams.

GOLDEN BALL: This award is given to the best player in the tournament, as determined by a vote by members of the media. The *Silver Ball* and *Bronze Ball* are awarded to the second and third best players, respectively.

GOLDEN BOOT: Awarded to the top goal scorer during the tournament. The *Golden Boot* is sometimes also called the *Golden Shoe*.

GOLDEN GLOVE AWARD: This is given to the best goalkeeper in the tournament. The winner is chosen by the FIFA Technical Study Group.

BEST YOUNG PLAYER AWARD: Given to the best player aged 21 or younger (at the start of the calendar year). This award is also chosen by the FIFA Technical Study Group.

FIFA FAIR PLAY TROPHY: Awarded to the team with the best record of fair play, a record determined by the points system and criteria established by the FIFA Fair Play Committee.

MOST ENTERTAINING TEAM: Until 2006, there was also an award given at the Men's World Cup to the team that most entertained the fans during the tournament. The winner was determined by a poll of the general public.

THE GAME THAT CHANGED EVERYTHING

ONE OF THE most memorable events in recent soccer history was the day the US Women's National team played China in the 1999 FIFA Women's World Cup. That year, the World Cup was held in the United States, and the US team was thrilled when they made it to the finals against China. There were a record number of fans at the game—more than at any other women's sporting event in history. 90,000 people crowded into the Rose Bowl in California to watch two superstar teams—and their star players, Mia Hamm and Sun Wen—compete for the championship. The game was tough and competitive, and ended scoreless after extra time. So the two teams prepared for a shootout to determine the winner.

China shot first and scored. But the US evened things up immediately when Carla Overbeck made the US team's first shot on goal. Joy Fawcett matched the second Chinese goal, keeping things even at 2–2. It was the third goal attempts where things got really exciting. first, the American goalkeeper, Briana Scurry, saved the Chinese player's shot. Then Kristine Lilly took a successful shot and the U.S. was up 3–2. China's fourth shot went in, but Mia Hamm answered with a goal of her own. When Sun Wen made the Chinese team's fifth and final shot, the teams were tied 4–4. The final US player, Brandi Chastain, made her way onto the field and put the ball past the Chinese keeper, clinching a US victory. Soccer fans in America celebrated a dramatic victory with the US National Team . . . and women's soccer came charging into the international sports world.

FANCY FOOTBALL

IN HONOR OF the 2010 World Cup in South Africa, a jewelry company made a special soccer ball that was crafted out of 6,620 white diamonds and 2,640 black diamonds. The regulation-size soccer ball weighed almost five pounds, had 3,500 carats of South African diamonds, and was worth $2.5 million dollars!

NO SHOES

IN 1950, INDIA backed out of the World Cup because players were required to wear shoes during the tournament—and their team wanted to play barefoot!

BLACK A·N·D WHITE BALL

D ID YOU KNOW that soccer balls were first made with the classic black-and-white checkerboard pattern for the 1970 FIFA World Cup? Around the world, most TVs were black-and-white then, and the checkered look was easier to see on people's TV sets.

THERE WERE ONLY 300 people at the first World Cup, which was held in Uruguay in 1930. Since then, things have really changed. At the 2010 World Cup in South Africa, more than 3 million spectators attended.

FIFA BALLON D'OR

THE FIFA BALLON d'Or (translated from French as "Golden Ball") is awarded to the top male soccer player of the year. Journalists, coaches, and captains of international teams vote to determine the winner of this prestigious award each year. The international Ballon d'Or was first given out in 2010, after the magazine *France Football*'s Ballon d'Or and the FIFA (Men's) World Player of the Year award were combined into one award. After Ballon d'Or and FIFA World Player of the Year were combined into one award for the top male player of the year, the title of FIFA World Player of the Year became a women-only award.

THE FIFA PLAYER of the Year Award is given each year to the woman voted best in the world by coaches and captains of teams around the world for the past season. The award was first given to Mia Hamm in 2001, and since then, a few players have dominated year after year.

- 2001: Mia Hamm (USA)
- 2002: Mia Hamm (USA)
- 2003: Birgit Prinz (Germany)
- 2004: Birgit Prinz (Germany)
- 2005: Birgit Prinz (Germany)
- 2006: Marta (Brazil)

- 2007: Marta (Brazil)
- 2008: Marta (Brazil)
- 2009: Marta (Brazil)
- 2010: Marta (Brazil)
- 2011: Homare Sawa (Japan)
- 2012: Abby Wambach (USA)
- 2013: Nadine Angerer (Germany)

SOCCER

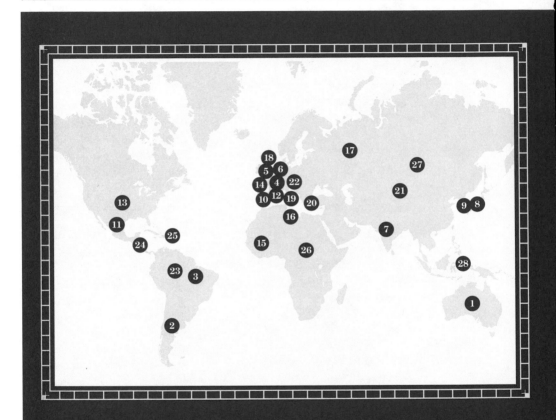

1. AUSTRALIA
2. ARGENTINA
3. BRAZIL
4. GERMANY
5. ENGLAND & WALES
6. NETHERLANDS
7. INDIA

8. JAPAN
9. SOUTH KOREA
10. SPAIN
11. MEXICO
12. FRANCE
13. UNITED STATES
14. PORTUGAL

15. SOUTH AFRICA
16. RWANDA
17. RUSSIA
18. SCOTLAND
19. ITALY
20. GREECE
21. CHINA

22. EUROPE
23. SOUTH AMERICA
24. CENTRAL AMERICA
25. CARIBBEAN
26. AFRICA
27. ASIA
28. OCEANA

E VERYONE KNOWS ABOUT the FIFA World Cup and Women's World Cup (if you didn't know much about the World Cup before you read this book, you probably do now). But did you know that the greatest players from each country also play for teams in different soccer leagues throughout the world, all of which have their own championship tournaments and playoffs?

AROUND THE WORLD

BELOW ARE JUST a few of the biggest soccer leagues around the world—some you may have heard of before, but many may be unfamiliar to you:

- **A-League Australian Football** (Australia)
- **Argentine Primera División** (Argentina)
- **Bundesliga** (Germany)
- **Campeonato Brasileiro Série A** (Brazil)
- **Barclay's Premier League** (England and Wales)
- **Eredivisie** (Netherlands)
- **Indian League** (India)
- **J. League Division 1** (Japan)
- **K-League** (South Korea)
- **La Liga** (Spain)
- **Liga MX** (Mexico)
- **Ligue 1** (France)
- **Major League Soccer** (United States)
- **National Women's Soccer League** (United States)
- **Premier Soccer League** (South Africa)
- **Primeira Liga** (Portugal)
- **Primus National Football League** (Rwanda)
- **Russian Premier League** (Russia)
- **Scottish Premier League** (Scotland)
- **Serie A** (Italy)
- **Superleague Greece** (Greece)
- **Super League** (China)

IN ADDITION TO each country-specific league, there are also several prestigious regional competitions in which the best teams in each country or region go head-to-head to be crowned in one of these larger competitions. Here are a few of the big ones:

- **UEFA Champions League** (Europe)
- **UEFA Women's Championship** (Europe Women)
- **UEFA Europa League** (Europe)
- **Copa América** (South America)
- **Copa Libertadores** (South America and Mexico)
- **Copa Libertadores de América de Fútbol Femenino** (South America & Mexico—Women)
- **CONCACAF Champions League Gold Cup** (North America, Central America, and the Caribbean)
- **CAF Champions League** (Africa)
- **AFC Champions League** (Asia)
- **OFC Champions League** (Oceania)

THEN THERE'S THE big one: The FIFA Club World Cup is a worldwide competition pitting the winners of the AFC Champions League, CONCACAF Champions League, CAF Champions League, Copa Libertadores, OFC Champions League, UEFA Champions League, and the host country's national champion against one another in a knockout competition.

CHAMPIONS LEAGUE

THE UEFA CHAMPIONS League—organized in 1955 by the Union of European Football Associations—is one of the most famous and popular club soccer competitions in Europe. Up to four of the top soccer clubs per country (five, beginning in the 2015–2016 season) in Europe's strongest national leagues participate in the annual competition. The UEFA Champions League was originally called the Champions League and was sometimes also referred to as the European Cup. Spain, England, and Italy have won the most championships overall. The winner of the UEFA Champions League qualifies for the UEFA Super Cup and the FIFA Club World Cup.

BEACH SOCCER

PLAYING SOCCER ON the beach has always been very popular. In Rio de Janeiro, Brazil, in the 1920s, informal rules for beach soccer were finally put into place. Like futsal, beach soccer is also a very fast form of the game. In fact, on average, there is a shot on goal every 30 seconds in a beach soccer match! Since the ball is so hard to control on sand, beach soccer players try to keep the ball in the air as much as possible. Beach soccer is played with bare feet, and players use their head a lot to pass and shoot.

FUTSAL

FUTSAL IS FIFA'S official form of indoor, five-a-side soccer. Futsal is a superfast game of soccer that is played with a smaller, heavier ball (because ordinary soccer balls are too big and bouncy for hard indoor floors). The first FIFA Futsal World Cup was held in the Netherlands in 1989.

SOCCER OFF THE WALLS . . . AND STREETS . . . AND SHIRTS

UNLIKE FUTSAL, FIFA'S official form of indoor soccer, other varieties of indoor soccer often use walls and boards instead of touchlines. The ball stays in play for longer periods of time (no throw-ins, goal kicks, or corner kicks), so the game moves very fast. Most indoor leagues in the United States play six-a-side, but in Britain, indoor soccer is usually played with five people on each team.

In street soccer, anything goes. Any spare plot of flat ground can be used for a field. Goals can be rigged up out of a few close trees, coats, chalk, or really anything that denotes a place to score a goal. There are usually no refs in street soccer, and rules are much more fluid than in official soccer matches. Street soccer is where many of the greatest players in the world got their start—paling around with friends on the street or in a local park or in someone's yard, playing for the love of the game and neighborhood pride.

S·U·P·E·R STADIUMS

THE COOLEST PLACES
TO WATCH (AND PLAY!) SOCCER

SOCCER FANS CAN probably find some sort of game to watch just about any day of the year, wherever they are in the world. But there are many amazing stadiums around the world that are especially cool places to really *experience* a professional soccer match. Whether these stadiums are intriguing because of their architecture, setting, history, or very dedicated (and often loud) fans, all of these famous venues are dream destinations for soccer-loving girls everywhere. Hopefully someday your travels will let you visit one or more of these places to watch some of the greatest teams in the world play.

Sapporo, Japan, gets a lot of snow every year, so the **Sapporo Dome**'s engineers had to find a way to build a field that would get enough sunlight to keep the grass-playing surface alive, while also being protected from several feet of snow. The field inside the Sapporo Dome actually slides in and out of the stadium, giving the grass fresh air and sunlight on nice days, but tucking it away when the weather is bad!

In Marina Bay, Singapore, there is a truly unique soccer field. **The Float at Marina Bay** is completely surrounded by water.

The **San Siro** stadium in Milan, Italy, can hold more than 85,000 screaming fans. And the fans who come to this stadium to watch the Italian soccer teams Internazionale and AC Milan play are definitely loud. The fans of these two huge clubs chant, wave big banners, and shoot flares after every goal. If you want to experience some of the most dedicated fans in the world, San Siro is definitely a great place to visit for a game.

Wembley Stadium in London is England's national stadium and has hosted some of the most famous matches in soccer history. The England national football team plays at Wembley Stadium, and the FA Cup is held here. Wembley was also the host stadium for the 2012 Olympic soccer finals.

In Portugal, the **Estádio Municipal de Braga** (nicknamed "The Quarry") has one incredible feature that sets it apart from every other stadium in the world—one end

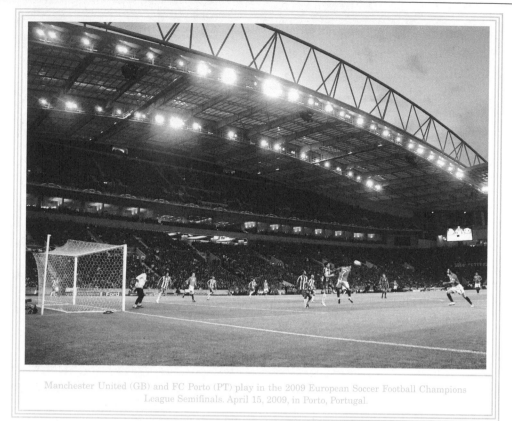

Manchester United (GB) and FC Porto (PT) play in the 2009 European Soccer Football Champions League Semifinals. April 15, 2009, in Porto, Portugal.

of the stadium butts up against a huge rock face. The stadium was carved into the face of the Monte Castro granite quarry!

- The **First National Bank Stadium** in Johannesburg, South Africa—which is sometimes called Soccer City—is nicknamed "The Calabash," because it looks a lot like the African pot of the same name (the pot is named after the calabash squash because it is shaped like one).The outside of the rounded stadium is made of a mosaic of fire and earthen colors, and the stadium almost glows when it is lit up at night. There is a ring of lights that runs around the bottom of the stadium, making it look like a fire is alight underneath the pot.

- The rounded **Allianz Arena** in Munich, Germany, is the only stadium in Europe that can change colors!

- Although the **Georgios Karaiskakis Stadium** in Athens, Greece, was completely renovated in 2004, it was originally constructed in 1896—making it one of the oldest stadiums in Greece and Europe.

- The **Olympiastadion** in Munich, Germany, was constructed in 1972 to host the Olympic Games. Today, it's the home of the Hertha BSC soccer team, and there are also some great music concerts held in this impressive stadium.

- The soccer final of the 2008 Olympics was played in the **Bird's Nest**, which is the nickname for the Beijing National Stadium in China. The stadium looks especially unique, since it is made of asymmetrical crisscrossed steel beams that make it look like a giant metal bird's nest.

Panoramic view of Camp Nou stadium before the Champions League match between FC Barcelona and A.C. Milan, final score 2–2, on September 13, 2011, in Barcelona, Spain.

The 2014 Olympics were held in Sochi, Russia, and the **Fisht Olympic Stadium** became the home base for the Russian National Football Team after the closing ceremonies. The stadium will also host some of the games in the 2018 World Cup, which is being held in Russia. The stadium's walls and roof are made of glass that reflects sunlight off the Black Sea during the day, and there is a view of mountain peaks and the sea from seats within the stadium itself.

In 2010, **Qatar** was selected to become the first Middle Eastern country to host the World Cup . . . in 2022. For a country with only 1.7 million people, this was a huge success—they beat out the United States, Australia, Japan, and South Korea to win the bid to host the tournament.

There are currently designs for five new stadiums for World Cup events in Qatar. Most of the new stadiums will be powered by sunlight, and each one of the proposed designs is incredibly unique. One stadium will have a giant screen on the outside of the stadium that will broadcast news and updates during the tournament. Another will be wrapped in colorful ribbons that represent the participating nations' colors. Another design was inspired by a seashell and looks like a giant eye from above. A fourth proposed design includes a pool, a spa area, and a shopping mall. The 2022 World Cup will definitely be a dream destination for soccer fans around the world!

I F YOU'RE SQUEAMISH, you might want to skip this section. Soccer is a pretty peaceful sport, but there have been a number of horrible tragedies that have taken place during soccer games over the past few centuries. Many times, angry fans or hooligans were to blame. Other times, a dangerous stadium has been at fault. Sometimes, the weather has been a soccer game's worst enemy. Here are a few of the worst soccer-related tragedies.

APRIL 5, 1902: **Glasgow, Scotland**
During a Scotland-England game, the back wall of the brand-new Ibrox Stadium was weakened by heavy rain the night before the match, and collapsed during the game. Hundreds of fans fell to the ground below. The stadium's gallery was rebuilt using concrete.

MARCH 9, 1946: **Manchester, England**
A mob of thousands of fans who were locked outside the stadium broke down the gates to force their way into the game. The stampede caused one wall of the stadium to collapse, and hundreds of people were injured or killed.

MAY 24, 1964: **Lima, Peru**
Hundreds of people died at an Olympic qualifying match between Peru and Argentina, when a protest over a rejected goal turned into a deadly fan riot.

SEPTEMBER 17, 1967: **Kayseri, Turkey**
During a passionate match between rivals Sivasspor Turkish Sports Club and Kayseri Erciyesspor Turkish Sports Club, a horrible fight broke out in the fan section that led to a riot that killed and injured more than 600 people.

JUNE 23, 1968: **Buenos Aires, Argentina**
When thousands of fans tried to leave the stadium through a closed exit door after the game, the people at the front of the crowd were accidentally crushed by people shoving at the back of the crowd.

JANUARY 2, 1971: **Glasgow, Scotland**
A second tragedy occurred at the Ibrox Stadium in Scotland when a portion of the stadium's structure collapsed, resulting in a huge pileup of spectators that left many people dead.

OCTOBER 20, 1982: Moscow, Russia

When a surprise goal was scored during extra time in the UEFA Cup match, fans who had already left the game turned and rushed back into the stadium. They collided with other fans who were trying to leave, and many people died.

MAY 11, 1985: Bradford, England

After a fan threw a lit cigarette behind his seat, it fell onto a huge pile of garbage under the wooden stands. The fire ignited quickly and burned down part of the wooden stadium while fans were trapped.

MARCH 12, 1988: Kathmandu, Nepal

Nearly 100 people were killed when fans tried to escape a powerful hailstorm. Only one stadium exit was open, so many people were crushed as they tried to rush for cover from the hail.

APRIL 15, 1989: Sheffield, England

When police officers opened one of the main gates, thousands of fans who were outside rushed to get into the stadium. The huge push of people led to many fans being crushed against riot fencing that had been put up to keep people back.

OCTOBER 16, 1996: Guatemala City, Guatemala

When fake tickets were sold before the game, 15,000 extra fans crowded into the stadium. This led to riots and a stampede of wild fans that killed nearly 100 people.

MAY 9, 2001: Accra, Ghana

When some crazed fans went wild and began tearing up seats and fighting, police fired tear gas into the stadium. 70,000 people tried to escape all at once, but all the gates had been locked during the game—this, plus the fighting, angry mob, killed 126 people.

FEBRUARY 1, 2012: Port Said, Egypt

Fans began fighting with sticks, rocks, and chairs, and this resulted in a huge riot that killed or injured thousands of bystanders.

HOOLIGANS & CRAZY FANS

THERE ARE DEFINITELY some crazy soccer fans around the world—and some of the craziest fans can get downright violent. A *football hooligan* is the name for a fan who gets violent, destructive, and out of control before, during, or after a match. Many fights have been started by hooligans, and they've also been known to vandalize property. Hooligans act out against the fans of opposing teams, and gangs of hooligans often get unruly and out of control, especially during heated and highly competitive matches and tournaments. Many soccer tragedies have occurred because of hooligans rioting in a stadium, but these violent fans also cause problems outside the stadium—such as setting fires around the city, smashing store or car windows, and creating chaos for fans who want to cheer for their team in a positive way.

INSPIRATIONAL SOCCER

THERE ARE MANY INCREDIBLE stories of teams and individuals around the world who have overcome obstacles or injury to prove that they can find a way to play soccer even in the most daunting situations. Teams and people overcome setbacks every day. In fact, there's a very good chance that your team will be faced with major challenges at some point during your soccer career, too. So I hope you'll be inspired by these amazing stories, and that you find the strength to stay positive in any situation.

KOH PANYEE
Football Club

I N THE SOUTH of Thailand, there is a floating village called Koh Panyee. Years ago, the children in this village loved to watch soccer and wanted to play, but since their houses and village were built on the water, there were no fields or open patches of land anywhere for them to make a field. But instead of letting that get in their way, they built their own field.

Using old fishing rafts and extra wood and nails, they created a floating soccer field. It was uneven and had nails sticking up all over, but it was a relatively flat place where the kids of this village could build teams and practice playing soccer. The ball—and the kids—fell into the water often, but the tight space and tricky surface helped the kids of Koh Panyee perfect their footwork so they could really control the ball.

One day, a kid on the team found out about a tournament on the mainland . . . and the team from Koh Panyee decided to enter. The rest of the village, proud of what the kids were doing, pitched in and bought them team jerseys and gear before their first big game. In that first tournament, the little team who played on a wooden raft went to the semifinals! Now, more than twenty years after that first raft was constructed, the Panyee Football Club is one of Thailand's best soccer clubs.

If you'd like more detail about this story, there is an excellent short video on YouTube that tells the story of the Koh Panyee football club.

URBAN MINISTRIES IN CHARLOTTE, NORTH CAROLINA

IN 2004, AN organization called Urban Ministries in Charlotte, North Carolina, decided to form a street soccer team made up of homeless individuals. The ministry believed that an organized soccer team would help some of the homeless people in their community get off the street by helping them live healthier, focus on a productive activity in their leisure time, and work with teammates toward a great goal.

The team worked incredibly hard to practice and perfect their game, and ended up winning the USA Street Soccer Championship. Also, in the program's first year, all eight of the team members found their way off the streets and into permanent housing, saying that their soccer program was the main reason they were able to escape homelessness.

Now, there is a soccer league with teams around the country that are made up of homeless people. Every year, a different country hosts the Homeless World Cup, where national teams of homeless players from different countries compete against one another. On the soccer field, everything is equal, and the only thing that matters is who practiced harder and believes they can do it—against all odds.

A SOCCER DYNASTY

THERE IS ONE college soccer team—and the coach who created it—that is especially famous for its women's soccer program: University of North Carolina at Chapel Hill (UNC). Since they began playing in the ACC Tournament in 1988, the Lady Tar Heels have been champions in all but five years. And since the first NCAA Women's Soccer Tournament in 1982, the Lady Tar Heels have won twenty-one of thirty-one championship games.

The North Carolina team is led by one of the most famous coaches in women's soccer, Anson Dorrance. He helped form the UNC women's soccer team in 1978, and in 1979, they became the first varsity women's soccer team in the southeast. Dorrance is known for recruiting top talent, and he has consistently developed an unstoppable team of women—including April Heinrichs, Shannon Higgins, Kristine Lilly, and Mia Hamm—who have gone on to play and coach professional soccer in European and American leagues.

NICO CALABRIA

BORN WITHOUT A hip and right leg, Nico Calabria of Concord, Massachusetts, decided early in life that he wasn't going to let anyone tell him what he could or couldn't do. When he was thirteen, Calabria first made headlines when he climbed Mount Kilimanjaro to raise money for charity (a five-and-a-half day journey)—using his single leg and a pair of crutches. Then he went on to wrestle and play soccer on his high school teams. Though he lacked some of the quickness of other players on the soccer field, he made up for it in skill.

In 2012, Calabria scored an incredible goal for his team, making him an instant celebrity with soccer fans around the world. The goal showcased his unique strength and talents—as the ball sailed over his teammate's head, Calabria used his leg, arm, and upper-body strength to twist in the air and kick the ball straight into the net with his leg up near his shoulders. A video of the goal was posted on YouTube, and people around the world have watched it more than a million times. Now, Calabria plays on the US National Amputee Soccer Team.

SOCCER FOR EVERYONE

S OCCER IS A popular sport for people with disabilities. There are many variations on the game that allow people with many different disabilities to enjoy the sport. Deaf soccer has been around for many years—Glasgow Deaf Athletic Football Club, the oldest deaf soccer club in the world, was founded in Scotland in 1871. There are also a number of people who play wheelchair soccer (using either manual or electric wheelchairs), and there are also leagues for amputee soccer (an amputee is someone who is missing one or more legs or arms).

In the Paralympics, there are actually two different soccer tournaments. In Paralympic seven-a-side soccer, the athletes who compete have all survived a traumatic brain injury, a stroke, or have cerebral palsy, meaning they have some impairment of muscular coordination. In Paralympic five-a-side soccer, the athletes have a visual impairment. The ball in Paralympic five-a-side has a special noisemaking device that helps the players figure out where the ball is. The only exception on the field: The goalkeepers are not visually impaired. Isn't it incredible that the players—who are either partially or completely blind, depending on the league—can score on a goalkeeper who can see everything?

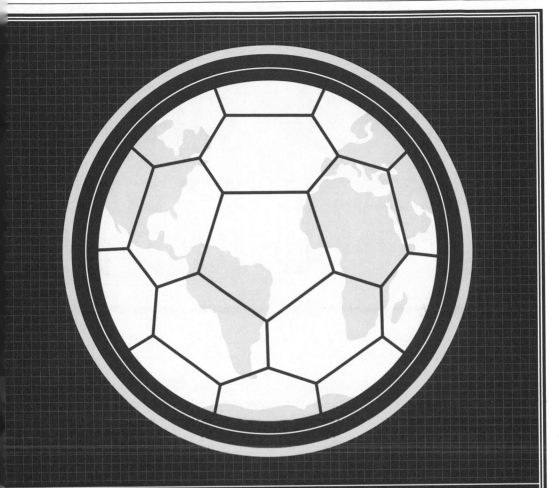

ONE WORLD FÚTBOL

EVERY YEAR, MANY soccer balls are donated to impoverished countries around the world so that children everywhere can enjoy soccer. Unfortunately, many times these balls deflate within hours or days, because they're often used on rocky dirt or rough fields—leaving children no choice but to go back to using homemade balls for their pickup games.

But several years ago, Tim Jahnigen invented a ball made out of PopFoam that won't go flat for thirty years—even in the worst conditions and on the roughest fields. Jahnigen got funding to develop the ball from the musician Sting, who named this incredible soccer ball the One World Ball. Though the One World Ball costs more to produce and ship than regular soccer balls, it allows children in more than 140 countries around the world to have fun playing soccer with their friends.

HOST A SUPER SOCCER PARTY

I F YOU LIVE and breathe soccer, what better way to celebrate your birthday than with a soccer-themed party? Even if your friends don't love soccer as much as you do (or even if they don't like it at all), you can have a great party where you share your passion for your favorite sport with your best buds. You could have a soccer party in your backyard, at a local park, or somewhere inside—your house, a gym, or even a rented sports facility—during the winter. Here are a few ideas to get you started:

Send out invitations that look like a ticket to a real soccer match.

Have everyone wear their favorite team jersey—you should probably have a few extra on hand for your non-soccer-playing friends. (Maybe you can even persuade your parents to dress up like referees!)

Decorate with colors and flags from your favorite team. To make it even more fun, make the decorations yourself.

Hang up pictures or posters of your favorite soccer players.

Paint everyone's face like a true soccer fan.

Make a playlist for your party with some of your favorite pregame pump-you-up songs!

Make some delicious soccer-themed snacks:
  soccer-ball cupcakes
  cookies that are decorated like soccer balls
  a cake that looks like a soccer field
  orange slices—just like the snacks at halftime during a real game

Serve drinks in water bottles or soccer stadium cups.

Turn the snack table into a soccer field—using just a green paper tablecloth and a white tape (to mark sidelines and goals).

Do some fun activities that make your favorite game the star of the party:
  pin the ball in the goal: A soccer-lover's version of pin the tail on the donkey!
  soccer ball juggling contests
  soccer piñata: Instead of breaking a piñata the usual way, tie a piñata (or taped-up paper bags full of candy) to a goal post—then let your guests take turns kicking the ball at it to try to get it to burst open!
  water balloon dribbling: fill a bunch of water balloons, then have a relay race to see who can dribble their filled balloon from Point A to Point B the fastest . . . without their ball popping! If it pops, start over at the beginning again.

BOOKS
TO GET YOU IN THE GAME

- *Go for the Goal* by Mia Hamm
- *Eyes on the Goal* by John Coy
- *The Kicks* (series) by Alex Morgan
- *Soccer Chick Rules* by Dawn Fitz-Gerald
- *Shoot-Out* by Mike Lupica
- *Pretty Tough* (series) by Nicole Leigh Shepherd
- *Outcasts United* by Warren St. John
- *Kickoff* by Donna King
- *Breakaway* by Andrea Montalbano
- *Soccer Hero* by Matt Christopher
- *Shut-Out!* by Camilla Reghelini Rivers
- *Soccer Spirit* by Jake Maddox
- *Just for Kicks* by Robert Rayner
- *Out of Sight* by Robert Rayner
- *Strikers: Young Blood* by David Ross
- *Breakaway* by Trevor Kew
- *Kickers* Series by Rich Wallace
- *Play On* by Sandra Diersch
- *Offside!* by Sandra Diersch
- *Trapped* by Michele Martin Bossley

GREAT MOVIES FOR SOCCER LOVERS

- *Her Best Move* (G)
- *The Game of Their Lives* (PG)
- *Soccer Dog: The Movie* (PG)
- *Soccer Dog: European Cup* (PG)
- *Bend It Like Beckham* (PG-13)
- *The Big Green* (PG)
- *Kicking & Screaming* (PG)
- *She's the Man* (PG-13)
- *Ladybugs* (PG-13)
- *Gracie* (PG-13)
- *Maradona by Kusturica* (Documentary)
- *Once in a Lifetime: The Extraordinary Story of the New York Cosmos* (Documentary)

tie-dyed jerseys: Everyone at your party gets to tie-dye special T-shirts, so you and your friends have matching jerseys for practice.

Movie Time: Rent or download an old World Cup game to watch, or chill out in front of one of your favorite soccer movies.

Rather than sending your friends away with ordinary party favors, share something really special with your BFFs—some fun soccer gear, such as:

hair ties

shirt bands (to tie back sleeves on hot days)

soccer ball key chains

a water bottle for practice

T-shirts that you and your friends make at the party together

personalized luggage tags for your friends to put on their soccer gear bag

soccer stadium cups

MIA WHO?

T·H·E

GREATEST

PLAYERS

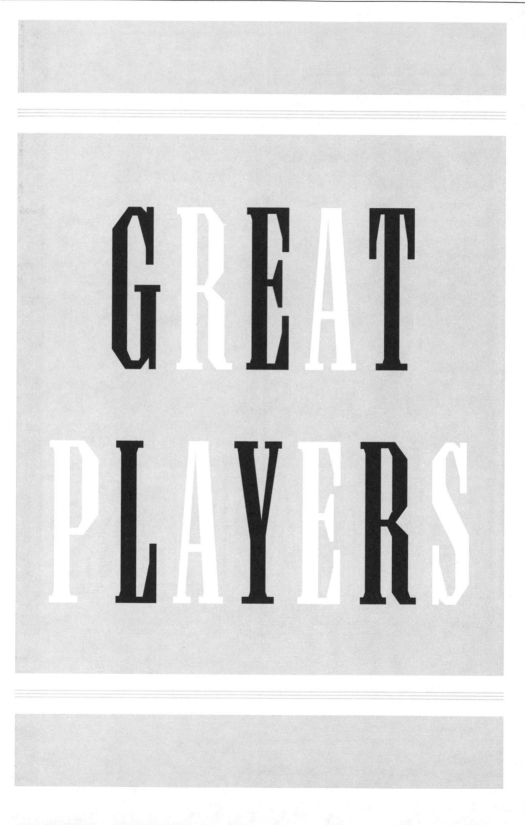

GREAT PLAYERS

ABBY WAMBACH

BORN:

- **June 2, 1980**

PLACE OF BIRTH:

- **Rochester, New York**

POSITION:

- **Forward**

E VERY GIRL IN America probably already knows that Mary Abigail "Abby" Wambach is a soccer superstar and a true inspiration for soccer-crazy girls. She's won the US Soccer Athlete of the Year award six times, and was named the FIFA Women's World Player of the Year in 2013. Wambach led the United States to a second-place finish at the 2011 Women's World Cup, and scored five goals in the 2012 Olympics on the way to a gold medal for the United States women's team.

Wambach—who is the youngest of seven kids—started playing soccer in a girls' youth league when she was four. But she was quickly switched from the girls' team to the boys' team after she scored 27 goals in just three games. She played both soccer and basketball in high school (she scored 142 goals during high school—34 of which were scored in 1997 alone), but began to focus on just soccer when she enrolled at the University of Florida. In 2002, she was drafted into the WUSA and joined Mia Hamm on the Washington Freedom. Hamm and Wambach made a great team, and Hamm became a very important mentor as Wambach continued to improve and perfect her game.

Wambach was invited to train with the US Women's National Team in 2003, and played with the team in the World Cup that year. Since that first World Cup match, she's gone on to become an international soccer phenomenon who is known around the world as one of the best players of all time.

MARTA

BORN:

February 19, 1986

PLACE OF BIRTH:

Dois Riachos, Alagoas, Brazil

POSITION:

Forward

M ARTA VIEIRA DA Silva, a Brazilian forward, is one of the most talented soccer players of all time. As a little girl growing up in a small town in Brazil, Marta was made fun of for wanting to play soccer with her brothers or the other neighborhood kids . . . because she was a girl. Soccer was known as a game for men and boys, so Marta was excluded. But she fought back and began to practice on the boys' team anyway, soon realizing that she had a huge soccer talent.

At the young age of fourteen, Marta was discovered by a famous coach and she moved from her village to the training facilities for Vasco da Gama, a soccer club in Rio de Janeiro. This is where she got her start as a professional soccer player. She began playing for the Brazilian national team in 2002. Since then, she's won the FIFA Women's World Player of the Year award a record five times in a row!

BIRGIT PRINZ

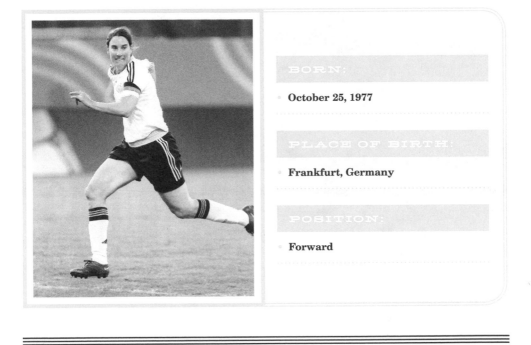

BORN:

• October 25, 1977

PLACE OF BIRTH:

• Frankfurt, Germany

POSITION:

• Forward

FEROCIOUS STRIKER BIRGIT Prinz led the German team to Women's World Cup titles in 2003 and 2007, before retiring from the game in 2011 after scoring 128 goals in 214 international games.

Growing up in Germany, Prinz loved sports. Her father was a soccer coach, and he suggested that she start playing soccer (her dad coached Prinz's youth team). When she was only sixteen, she made her international soccer debut for the German national team when she was brought onto the field as a substitute at the very end of the game. She scored the game-winning goal with just minutes left to play. She went on to play in her first World Cup for Germany when she was seventeen.

Prinz was the first player other than Mia Hamm to win the FIFA Women's World Player of the Year award. After winning Player of the Year for the first time in 2003, she went on to win it again the next two years in a row (and then came in second—behind Marta—for the next four years). She was also the top scorer at the Women's World Cup in 2003 and 2007.

CRISTIANE

- May 15, 1985

- Osasco, São Paulo, Brazil

- Forward

BRAZILIAN SOCCER STAR Cristiane Rozeira de Souza Silva (better known as just Cristiane) knew she wanted to be a soccer star when she was just seven years old, but there weren't any leagues available for girls in Brazil. So she started out playing pickup games with the boys who lived in her neighborhood. When she was fifteen, she began playing for the Brazil U-19 team. She joined the Brazilian national team as a substitute at the 2003 Women's World Cup, and then helped her country win a silver medal at both the 2004 and 2008 Olympics.

A big part of Cristiane's success on the field is her excellent partnership with the other Brazilian superstar, Marta. The two women are teammates on the Brazilian national team, and they also played together for the Chicago Red Stars. They always work together as an inspiring partnership.

KELLY SMITH

BORN:

• October 29, 1978

PLACE OF BIRTH:

• Watford, England

POSITION:

• Forward

KELLY SMITH STARTED playing soccer for the England team in 1995, just three days after she turned seventeen years old. As a child, she played on boys' teams . . . until she was kicked out of the boys' club at age seven, because other parents in the league complained. She went on to play for Pinner Girls, a soccer team that her father formed.

After her debut with the English women's team, she moved to the United States to play college soccer for Seton Hall University, where she broke multiple records (the school retired her jersey when she graduated). Since then, Smith has played for several professional teams, but most of her career has been spent leading the Arsenal team in England to victory in hundreds of matches around the world.

Smith is England's all-time leading scorer, despite suffering many injuries during her career.

HOMARE SAWA

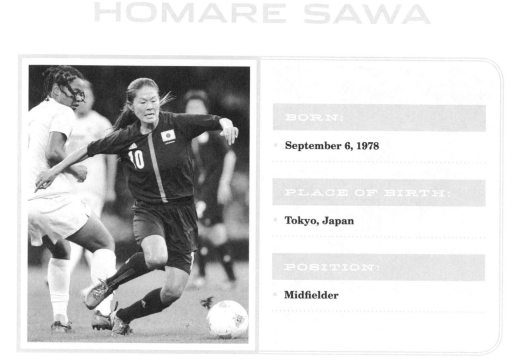

BORN:

• **September 6, 1978**

PLACE OF BIRTH:

• **Tokyo, Japan**

POSITION:

• **Midfielder**

S OCCER LOVERS EVERYWHERE knew the name Homare Sawa after she led her Japanese team to the 2011 Women's World Cup title, beating the United States in a dramatic penalty shootout. During the tournament, she led scoring and earned the Golden Ball trophy as the best player. To cap off a great year, she was chosen as the FIFA Women's World Player of the Year in 2012 (beating Marta, who had won for the past five years in a row).

Sawa first started playing professional soccer in Japan's first division when she was just a tiny twelve-year-old. When she was fifteen, she joined the Japanese national team and scored four goals in her first match with the team. Just a few months after she was awarded World Player of the Year and after she helped lead the Japanese team to a silver medal at the 2012 Olympics, she announced her retirement. She will always be known as one of the greatest players ever to play for Japan.

HANNA LJUNGBERG

HANNA LJUNGBERG

BORN:

• **January 8, 1979**

PLACE OF BIRTH:

• **Umeå, Sweden**

POSITION:

• **Forward**

HANNA LJUNGBERG IS one of the most famous Swedish soccer players in history. During her twelve years of play on the Swedish team (1996–2008), Ljungberg scored 72 goals for Sweden. She also helped lead Sweden to a second-place finish at the 2003 Women's World Cup.

Though she was a forward, she stepped in to play goalkeeper in the 70th minute of the 2007 Swedish Cup, when the team's first-string goalkeeper was injured. Ljungberg retired in 2008, after suffering a serious knee injury.

KRISTINE LILLY

BORN:

• July 22, 1971

PLACE OF BIRTH:

• New York, New York

POSITION:

• Forward/Midfielder

KRISTINE LILLY IS one of the best-known names in American women's soccer. She retired from the Boston Breakers in 2011 after playing professional soccer for more than fifteen years. While she was still playing high school soccer, Lilly was invited to join the United States Women's National Team. After high school, she was recruited to the prestigious college soccer team at the University of North Carolina Chapel Hill.

After college, she joined the Tyreso FF professional soccer team in Sweden. After just one season, she returned to the United States to become the only woman on an all-male team in a professional indoor soccer league. In 2001, she was one of the founding members and the team captain for the brand-new Boston Breakers team in the Women's United Soccer Association (WUSA). When the WUSA folded, Lilly returned to Sweden until the Boston Breakers were reformed as part of the Women's Professional Soccer League.

In her long and successful career, Lilly participated in five Women's World Cups and medaled in three Olympic Games. She will always be celebrated as one of the most important and greatest American soccer players. Now, Lilly runs a summer soccer academy where young players can learn from some of the best soccer players in the country.

RENATE LINGOR

BORN:

• October 11, 1975

PLACE OF BIRTH:

• Karlsruhe, Germany

POSITION:

• Midfielder

MIDFIELDER RENATE LINGOR didn't score lots of goals during her career—but she did help the German team win two Women's World Cup tournaments, five German league titles, and five German Cup crowns in her twelve years of professional soccer. She also scored the game-winning goal to secure the bronze medal for Germany at the 2004 Olympics.

Lingor began playing soccer when she was six years old, and got her start in professional soccer—playing for German team SC Klinge Seckach—when she was only fourteen. Even though she got offers from many of the best German teams, she stayed with that team until 1997 when she signed with FFC Frankfurt. Lingor retired in 2008 after a great career as a German soccer star.

SUN WEN

BORN:

○ April 6, 1973

PLACE OF BIRTH:

○ Shanghai, China

POSITION:

○ Forward

CHINESE FORWARD SUN Wen won the Golden Boot and Golden Ball as the top scorer and best player of the 1999 Women's World Cup. She scored 106 goals in 152 international matches before retiring in 2006.

She began playing soccer when she was eleven, partly because her father loved the sport and encouraged her to play. She earned a spot on the Chinese women's national team at the age of seventeen. Many people believed that she was a better player than Mia Hamm, who was one of America's greatest players during Sun Wen's years on the Chinese team.

The only thing missing from her incredible career? A World Cup title. The Chinese team came close . . . but lost to the United States during a historic and memorable penalty shootout in the 1999 tournament.

TIFFENY MILBRETT

BORN:

October 23, 1972

PLACE OF BIRTH:

Portland, Oregon

POSITION:

Forward

TIFFENY MILBRETT WAS one of the greatest American soccer players of the 1990s and 2000s. She started playing in her local neighborhood club as a kid, and her mom was her coach. When she was only ten, Milbrett also regularly stepped into her mother's women's soccer league games as a sub when one of the team's players failed to show! She was a star on the soccer team in high school, but she was also very successful at basketball and track and field—in fact, she was offered college scholarships for both of those sports.

But Milbrett chose soccer, and in college at the University of Oregon, she stood out as one of the best players on the team. She played her first game with the US U-20 team in 1991 while she was still in college. When she graduated from college, soccer became Milbrett's career. She joined a professional soccer team in Japan after she graduated, and also joined the US Senior Women's National Team. She became a starter on the US Women's National Team in 1996—the year the team won the gold medal at the Olympics—and played for the US team for fifteen years.

Milbrett was one of the players who helped get the WUSA up and running and played a huge part in American women's soccer until she retired from the game in 2011.

SHANNON BOXX

BORN:

° June 29, 1977

PLACE OF BIRTH:

° Fontana, California

POSITION:

° Midfielder

A S A TEENAGER, Shannon Boxx played for the Torrance United Waves Soccer Club in her hometown of Fontana, California. Her competitive team played in four state championships and two national championships in the years she was on the team. While she was playing for her club team, Boxx also played for her high school. She was a standout on the soccer field, but also played volleyball, softball, and basketball. Her sister also played softball—in fact, Boxx's sister won a gold medal in softball at the 1996 Olympics!

Boxx went to college at Notre Dame, where she was on the honor roll. She helped lead her team to their first NCAA Women's Soccer Championship when she was just a freshman. When she graduated in 1999, she played for a very short while on a Boston team, then joined a German professional team. She considered retiring from soccer and going to graduate school, because she was unhappy after her first few seasons—but then the WUSA was formed, and she was drafted to the San Diego Spirit.

It wasn't until she had graduated from college and began playing in the WUSA that Boxx joined the US Women's National Team in 2003, just in time for the FIFA Women's World Cup. She was the first player ever to be named to a World Cup team without ever playing a match with the squad! She continued to shine on the US Women's National Team, but had to sit out most of the 2006 season after she was injured. She returned at full strength in 2007 for the next World Cup and the 2008 Olympics. She currently plays for the Chicago Red Stars and is known as one of the best defensive midfielders ever to play for the United States.

ALEX MORGAN

BORN:

• July 2, 1989

PLACE OF BIRTH:

• Diamond Bar, California

POSITION:

• Forward (#13)

ALEXANDRA "ALEX" MORGAN was a talented all-around athlete when she was a kid, but she didn't start playing in an organized soccer league until she was fourteen. Amazingly, only three years later, she joined the National U-17 team. She also played for her high school soccer team, and then went on to play for University of California-Berkeley. She was as committed to school as she is to soccer, and was able to graduate from college with a degree in political economy a full semester early.

Morgan became the youngest member of the US Women's National Team while she was still in college, and played with the team in the 2011 FIFA Women's World Cup. In 2011, she was also drafted first in the Women's Professional Soccer draft and joined the Western New York Flash. When the WPS league shut down at the end of the 2011 season, she played on the United Soccer League's W-League. Morgan and the US Women's National Team went on to win a gold medal at the 2012 Olympics, after Morgan scored the game-winning goal in the semifinal match against Canada in extra time. In 2013, she joined the Portland Thorns in the Women's National Soccer League.

Morgan is a brilliant soccer player but she has a lot of other interests as well. She loves tennis (watching and playing), snowboarding, wakeboarding, and yoga. She also finds time to write books for kids—her new fiction series is called *The Kicks*, and the first book came out in 2013.

HOPE SOLO

BORN

- July 30, 1981

PLACE OF BIRTH

- Richland, Washington

POSITION

- Goalkeeper

HOPE SOLO IS an incredible goalkeeper for the United States's National Team—but she actually started her soccer career as a forward on her high school team. It wasn't until college at the University of Oregon that she switched over to keeper, and it's proven to be a great move for her.

Solo began playing with the US Senior National Team in 2000 while she was still in college. She was named to the United States Olympic team in 2004 as an alternate, and became the team's first choice goalkeeper starting in 2005. She was the United States's star goal keeper during the 2008 and 2012 Olympics, helping her team take gold in both games. She also received the Golden Glove award during the 2011 Women's World Cup, after the US team took second in the competition.

Her best goalkeeping streak? She once went 1,094 minutes without letting a goal get past her! She's also an excellent dancer . . . Solo made it to the semifinals on *Dancing With the Stars* in 2011.

MIA HAMM

BORN:

• March 17, 1972

PLACE OF BIRTH:

• Selma, Alabama

POSITION:

• Forward

NO FEMALE PLAYER has had a bigger impact on women's soccer than Mariel Margaret "Mia" Hamm. During her long and championship-filled career, Hamm scored more international goals than any other player—male or female—in the history of the game. Mia Hamm also changed the way people around the world view women's soccer.

Mia Hamm's father was an Air Force pilot, so she and her family moved around a lot throughout her childhood. Though she was born with a clubfoot and had to wear special corrective casts as a baby, she began playing soccer when she was just four or five years old. She was one of six kids, and her older brother Garrett encouraged her love of sports. By the time she was fifteen, Hamm was already playing for the United States National Team! She played college soccer at University of North Carolina at Chapel Hill, and while she was a Tar Heel, the team won four consecutive NCAA championships.

Twice the FIFA World Player of the Year, Hamm led the US team to World Cup titles in 1991 and 1999, and she also won Olympic gold in 1996 and 2004. Hamm retired in 2004 after an amazing soccer career that saw the birth of a women's professional league in the United States, and inspired millions of girls to start playing soccer.

PELÉ

- **BORN: October 23, 1940**
- **PLACE OF BIRTH: Três Corações, Brazil**
- **POSITION: Forward**

E DSON ARANTES DO Nascimento—known as Pelé—is often considered the greatest soccer player of all time. He grew up poor and developed his soccer skills by kicking a sock stuffed with rags around the streets near his house. Eventually, he joined a kids' team that was coached by a former member of the Brazilian national team. Pelé got his big break at age fifteen, when he tried out for and was offered a position on the Santos professional soccer club.

He played professional soccer for more than twenty years, and his Brazilian team won the World Cup in 1958, 1962, and 1970. Even though Pelé got offers to join a number of European soccer clubs, the president of Brazil declared him a "national treasure," making it impossible for him to play for another country's team. During his career, Pelé scored 1,281 goals in 1,363 games! He was named as the FIFA co-Player of the Century (together with Diego Maradona) in 1999. After he retired from the great game, Pelé turned his focus to great causes—he was awarded the International Peace Award for his work with UNICEF, and he was also a United Nations ambassador for ecology and the environment.

LIONEL MESSI

- **BORN: June 24, 1987**
- **PLACE OF BIRTH: Rosario, Argentina**
- **POSITION: Forward**

M ANY PEOPLE BELIEVE that Lionel Andrés Messi—known as Leo—will easily top Pelé for the title of greatest soccer player of all time. Though he was born in Argentina, Messi moved to Spain when he was thirteen after the FC Barcelona soccer club offered to pay for expensive hormone-deficiency treatments for the promising young soccer player (Messi had always been smaller than other kids his age, and doctors discovered that he had a hormone deficiency that restricted his growth). Shortly after he moved

to Spain, Messi joined FC Barcelona's youth team, and became a star in his new country. When he was just seventeen, Messi became the youngest player ever to score a goal for the FC Barcelona's senior team.

Over the next few years, Messi became an international superstar. He has played in two World Cups for his native Argentina, and he helped the Argentinian team take home an Olympic gold medal in 2008. During the 2012 season, Messi broke the record for most goals scored in a single year—91 goals in club and international play—beating the old record of 85! He won the FIFA Ballon d'Or award in 2009, 2010, 2011, and 2012—a record-breaking four years in a row—and he doesn't show any sign of slowing down anytime soon.

DIEGO MARADONA

- **BORN: October 30, 1960**
- **PLACE OF BIRTH: Buenos Aires, Argentina**
- **POSITION: Midfielder**

DIEGO ARMANDO MARADONA is one of the greatest dribblers in the history of soccer. He got his first soccer ball as a gift when he was three, and fell in love with the game as a young kid. When he was ten, Maradona joined a youth team in one of the biggest soccer clubs in Argentina. He made his professional debut when he was just fifteen!

Maradona's most memorable goal was scored during the 1986 World Cup. In the quarterfinal game, he appeared to head the ball—but it was actually his hand that helped lead the ball into the net. Maradona claimed that it hadn't been his hand, but rather that the goal had been scored "a little with the head of Maradona, and a little with the hand of God." Before he retired in 1997, Maradona played in four World Cups and was named FIFA co-player of the Century in 1999 (together with Pelé).

CRISTIANO RONALDO

- **BORN: February 5, 1985**
- **PLACE OF BIRTH: Funchal, Madeira, Portugal**
- **POSITION: Forward**

CRISTIANO RONALDO DOS Santos Aveiro is easily one of the best players to grace the pitch in recent years. He holds many scoring records, and has been paid record sums of money to play for some of the biggest and best soccer clubs in the world.

Cristiano Ronaldo loved soccer as a kid, and spent hours playing his favorite game. He played for youth clubs in Portugal and got his professional start with several clubs in his native country. He joined the Portuguese senior national team in 2003, and that same year he signed with Manchester United in England to become the team's first-ever Portuguese player. He wore number seven for Manchester United, the jersey worn by some of the best players in club history, including David Beckham and George Best. After several years, he was wooed away from Manchester United and joined Real Madrid in 2009—they paid a record $131 million for him!

Ronaldo was awarded the Ballon d'Or Award for the 2008 season. In January 2014, he won again for the 2013 season—becoming the first person to beat Lionel Messi for the award since 2009.

ZINEDINE ZIDANE

- **BORN:** June 23, 1972
- **PLACE OF BIRTH:** Marseille, France
- **POSITION:** Midfielder

Z INEDINE YAZID ZIDANE was one of the greatest soccer players in the world during the late 1990s and early 2000s. He was born in France to Algerian immigrant parents. He grew up playing soccer in the streets, and starred on several youth clubs before he was discovered at the age of fourteen by a recruiter for the AS Cannes team. He made his professional debut when he was just seventeen.

Zidane won the FIFA World Player of the Year award three times, before retiring from play in 2006. The final game of his career was during the 2006 World Cup finals between Italy and Spain—unfortunately, Zidane was kicked out of the game after headbutting an Italian player, and his team went on to lose the game.

GEORGE WEAH

- **BORN:** October 1, 1966
- **PLACE OF BIRTH:** Monrovia, Liberia
- **POSITION:** Forward

G EORGE WEAH IS as famous for his humanitarian efforts as he is for his soccer skills. Born into extreme poverty, Weah was raised by his grandmother in one of the roughest neighborhoods in all of Monrovia. He began playing soccer for the Young Survivors team when he was fifteen, and when he was twenty-two, Weah was noticed by the coach of the Cameroon National team. He'd had almost no formal training, but he was offered a chance to play for AS Monaco. He quickly turned into a true force on the field, and his talent grew when he switched over to a Paris team. By the end of the 1994–95 season, Weah had become a legend—and he was named the African, European, and FIFA World Player of the Year.

During his rise to fame, Weah never forgot where he came from. He has continually worked to try to improve conditions in his war-torn home country; he's been active in HIV/AIDS awareness programs; and he has also spent a lot of his own money to support the Liberian national team. After he retired from soccer, Weah ran for Liberia's presidency. Though he lost the election, he remains an incredibly influential figure in Liberia and currently works as a peace ambassador for his home nation.

JOHAN CRUYFF

- **BORN: April 25, 1947**
- **PLACE OF BIRTH: Amsterdam, The Netherlands**
- **POSITION: Forward**

D UTCH PLAYER HENDRIK Johannes Cruijff (best known as Johan Cruyff) was a star player for Ajax and Barcelona in the 1960s and 1970s, and is considered to be Europe's best soccer player of all time. He got his start playing for Ajax in the Netherlands, where he led his team to the Dutch championship six times.

In the 1974 World Cup, Cruyff was an important part of the new Dutch "Total Football" movement. Total Football was a new style of play in which players interchanged positions on the field. Because he participated in this new soccer philosophy, Cruyff was successful in many different positions—and is best known for his exceptional pass timing—which is part of what led to his long and successful career. After he retired from the game in 1984, Cruyff went on to lead Ajax and FC Barcelona as a highly successful manager.

FRANZ BECKENBAUER

- **BORN: September 11, 1945**
- **PLACE OF BIRTH: Munich, Germany**
- **POSITION: Midfielder/Defender**

F RANZ BECKENBAUER—nicknamed "The Kaiser" or "The Emperor"—is the only man in history who has won the World Cup as both a team captain and a coach.

In the early 1970s, Beckenbauer first made history when he switched from a central midfield position to an attacking sweeper role. He was an expert at moving play from the back, dribbling the ball up the field, and joining his team's offense. He invented the role of attacking sweeper, and his elegance and element of surprise on the field made him famous—and lethal.

The West German team won the World Cup in 1974 when Beckenbauer was the captain, and his team also won three league titles and three European Cups from 1974 to 1976. After he retired from play, Beckenbauer went on to coach—and he led his German team to another World Cup victory in 1990 as manager.

ALFREDO DI STÉFANO

- **BORN:** July 4, 1926
- **PLACE OF BIRTH:** Buenos Aires, Argentina
- **POSITION:** Midfielder/Forward

T HOUGH ALFREDO STÉFANO Di Stéfano Laulhé was one of the most important players for Real Madrid in the 1950s and 1960s (he even acquired Spanish citizenship so he could play for the Spanish National team), he never played in a World Cup. However, his Real Madrid team won the European Cup five times in a row while he was on the team, and Di Stéfano scored in every single one of the final matches of each of those tournaments.

Di Stéfano—nicknamed "Saeta Rubia" (Blond Arrow)—was a versatile player, and he was successful as a defender, an attacking midfielder, and a forward. For many years, he held the record for highest scorer in Spanish history, having scored 216 goals in 282 matches over eleven years.

BOBBY CHARLTON

- **BORN:** October 11, 1937
- **PLACE OF BIRTH:** Ashington, Northumberland, England
- **POSITION:** Midfielder

S IR ROBERT "BOBBY" Charlton began playing professional soccer when he was just fifteen—which is not surprising, considering he was born into a soccer family. His mother taught all her kids to play and encouraged Charlton's love of the sport. Even though he was born with soccer blood, his parents were concerned about a teenager committing himself fully to soccer, so Charlton also became an electrical engineering apprentice to ensure he had a backup plan.

Charlton was one of the most influential players for Manchester United in the fifties and sixties, and he was also a member of the England team who won the World Cup in 1966. He was the first soccer player in English history to play in four World Cups, and is widely regarded as one of the most professional and courteous players on the field. He rarely argued with refs and was always respectful to other players on the field. For his service, he was knighted by the queen of England in 1994.

NATIONAL WOMEN'S SOCCER LEAGUE AWARDS 2013

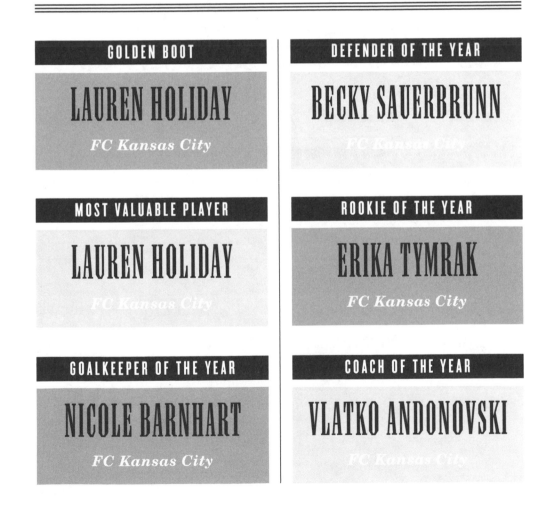

GOLDEN BOOT

LAUREN HOLIDAY

FC Kansas City

DEFENDER OF THE YEAR

BECKY SAUERBRUNN

FC Kansas City

MOST VALUABLE PLAYER

LAUREN HOLIDAY

FC Kansas City

ROOKIE OF THE YEAR

ERIKA TYMRAK

FC Kansas City

GOALKEEPER OF THE YEAR

NICOLE BARNHART

FC Kansas City

COACH OF THE YEAR

VLATKO ANDONOVSKI

FC Kansas City

NWSL

BEST XI 2013

POSITION	PLAYER	CLUB
GOALKEEPER	Nicole Barnhart	FC Kansas City
DEFENDER	Christie Rampone	Sky Blue FC
DEFENDER	Leigh Ann Robinson	FC Kansas City
DEFENDER	Becky Sauerbrunn	FC Kansas City
DEFENDER	Brittany Taylor	Western New York Flash
MIDFIELDER	Lori Chalupny	Chicago Red Stars
MIDFIELDER	Jess Fishlock	Seattle Reign FC
MIDFIELDER	Lauren Holiday	FC Kansas City
MIDFIELDER	Diana Matheson	Washington Spirit
FORWARD	Sydney Leroux	Boston Breakers
FORWARD	Abby Wambach	Western New York Flash

NWSL

SECOND XI 2013

POSITION	PLAYER	CLUB
GOALKEEPER	Adrianna Franch	Western New York Flash
DEFENDER	Rachel Buehler	Portland Thorns
DEFENDER	Caitlin Foord	Sky Blue FC
DEFENDER	Ali Krieger	Washington Spirit
DEFENDER	Lauren Sesselmann	FC Kansas City
MIDFIELDER	Megan Rapinoe	Seattle Reign FC
MIDFIELDER	Desiree Scott	FC Kansas City
MIDFIELDER	Erika Tymrak	FC Kansas City
FORWARD	Alex Morgan	Portland Thorns
FORWARD	Liane Sanderson	Boston Breakers
FORWARD	Christine Sinclair	Portland Thorns

U.S. WOMEN'S NATIONAL TEAM RECORDS

TOP TEN MOST CAPPED PLAYERS

1. KRISTINE LILLY
Caps: 352 • Goals: 130

2. CHRISTIE RAMPONE
Caps: 291 • Goals: 4

3. MIA HAMM
Caps: 275 • Goals: 158

4. JULIE FOUDY
Caps: 272 • Goals: 45

5. JOY FAWCETT
Caps: 239 • Goals: 27

6. ABBY WAMBACH
Caps: 220 • Goals: 167

7. TIFFENY MILBRETT
Caps: 204 • Goals: 100

8. KATE MARKGARF
Caps: 202 • Goals: 1

9. HEATHER O'REILLY
Caps: 202 • Goals: 40

10. BRANDI CHASTAIN
Caps: 192 • Goals: 30

TOP TEN GOAL SCORERS

1. ABBY WAMBACH
Caps: 220 • Goals: 167

2. MIA HAMM
Caps: 275 • Goals: 158

3. KRISTINE LILLY
Caps: 352 • Goals: 130

4. MICHELLE AKERS
Caps: 153 • Goals: 105

5. TIFFENY MILBRETT
Caps: 204 • Goals: 100

6. CINDY PARLOW
Caps: 158 • Goals: 75

7. SHANNON MACMILLAN
Caps: 176 • Goals: 60

8. CARIN JENNINGS-GABARRA
Caps: 117 • Goals: 53

9. CARLI LLOYD
Caps: 170 • Goals: 50

10. JULIE FOUDY
Caps: 272 • Goals: 45

TOP TEN ASSISTS

1. MIA HAMM
Caps: 275 • Assists: 144

2. KRISTINE LILLY
Caps: 352 • Assists: 105

3. ABBY WAMBACH
Caps: 220 • Assists: 67

4. TIFFENY MILBRETT
Caps: 204 • Assists: 61

5. JULIE FOUDY
Caps: 272 • Assists: 55

6. SHANNON MACMILLAN
Caps: 176 • Assists: 50

7. HEATHER O'REILLY
Caps: 202 • Assists: 50

8. CARIN JENNINGS-GABARRA
Caps: 117 • Assists: 47

9. ALY WAGNER
Caps: 131 • Assists: 42

10. MICHELLE AKERS
Caps: 153 • Assists: 36

WORLD CUP AWARDS

T HE GOLDEN BALL is given to the best player at the World Cup final every four years. The second- and third-best players in the tournament are awarded the Silver Ball and Bronze Ball, respectively.

1991 WORLD CUP IN CHINA

GOLDEN BALL:
Carin Jennings (United States)

Michelle Akers (United States)

BRONZE BALL:
Linda Medalen (United States)

1995 WORLD CUP IN SWEDEN

GOLDEN BALL:
Hege Riise (Norway)

Gro Espeseth (Norway)

BRONZE BALL:
Ann Kristin Aarones (Norway)

1999 WORLD CUP IN THE UNITED STATES

GOLDEN BALL:
Sun Wen (China)

Sissi (Brazil)

BRONZE BALL:
Michelle Akers (United States)

2003 WORLD CUP IN THE UNITED STATES

GOLDEN BALL:
Birgit Prinz (Germany)

Victoria Svensson (Sweden)

BRONZE BALL:
Maren Meinert (Germany)

2007 WORLD CUP IN CHINA

GOLDEN BALL:
Marta (Brazil)

Birgit Prinz (Germany)

BRONZE BALL:
Cristiane (Brazil)

2011 WORLD CUP IN JAPAN

GOLDEN BALL:
Homare Sawa (Japan)

Abby Wambach (United States)

BRONZE BALL:
Hope Solo (United States)

US WOMEN'S NATIONAL TEAM

US WOMEN'S OLYMPIC TEAM 2012	US WOMEN'S OLYMPIC TEAM 2008
Nicole Barnhart, *Goalkeeper*	Nicole Barnhart, *Goalkeeper*
Shannon Boxx, *Midfield*	Hope Solo, *Goalkeeper*
Rachel Buehler, *Defense*	Rachel Buehler, *Defense*
Lauren Cheney, *Forward*	Lori Chalupny, *Defense*
Tobin Heath, *Midfield*	Stephanie Cox, *Defense*
Amy LePeilbet, *Defense*	Kate Markgraf, *Defense*
Sydney Leroux, *Forward*	Heather Mitts, *Defense*
Carli Lloyd, *Midfield*	Christie Rampone, *Defense*
Heather Mitts, *Defense*	Shannon Boxx, *Midfield*
Alex Morgan, *Forward*	Tobin Heath, *Midfield*
Kelley O'Hara, *Forward*	Angela Hucles, *Midfield*
Heather O'Reilly, *Forward*	Carli Lloyd, *Midfield*
Christie Rampone, *Defense*	Heather O'Reilly, *Midfield*
Megan Rapinoe, *Forward*	Lindsay Tarpley, *Midfield*
Amy Rodriguez, *Forward*	Aly Wagner, *Midfield*
Becky Sauerbrunn, *Defense*	Natasha Kai, *Forward*
Hope Solo, *Goalkeeper*	Amy Rodriguez, *Forward*
Abby Wambach, *Forward*	Abby Wambach, *Forward*

OLYMPIC SQUAD

US WOMEN'S OLYMPIC TEAM

Kristin Luckenbill, *Goalkeeper*

Briana Scurry, *Goalkeeper*

Brandi Chastain, *Defense*

Joy Fawcett, *Defense*

Kate Markgraf, *Defense*

Heather Mitts, *Defense*

Christie Rampone, *Defense*

Cat Reddick, *Defense*

Shannon Boxx, *Midfield*

Julie Foudy, *Midfield*

Angela Hucles, *Midfield*

Kristine Lilly, *Midfield*

Lindsay Tarpley, *Midfield*

Aly Wagner, *Midfield*

Mia Hamm, *Forward*

Heather O'Reilly, *Forward*

Cindy Parlow, *Forward*

Abby Wambach, *Forward*

US WOMEN'S OLYMPIC TEAM 2000

Michelle French, *Defense*

Brandi Chastain, *Defense*

Lorrie Fair, *Midfielder*

Joy Fawcett, *Defense*

Julie Foudy, *Midfield*

Mia Hamm, *Forward*

Kristine Lilly, *Midfield*

Shannon MacMillan, *Midfield*

Tiffeny Milbrett, *Forward*

Siri Mullinix, *Goalkeeper*

Carla Overbeck, *Defense*

Cindy Parlow, *Forward*

Christine Pearce, *Defense*

Briana Scurry, *Goalkeeper*

Nikki Serlenga, *Midfield*

Danielle Slaton, *Defense*

Kate Sobrero, *Defense*

Sara Whalen, *Midfield*

YEAR	PLACE	PLAYER	NATIONALITY	CLUB
2001	1st	Mia Hamm	United States	Washington Freedom
	2nd	Tiffeny Milbrett	United States	New York Power
	3rd	Sun Wen	China PR	Atlanta Beat
2002	1st	Mia Hamm	United States	Washington Freedom
	2nd	Birgit Prinz	Germany	1. FFC Frankfurt
	3rd	Sun Wen	China PR	Atlanta Beat
2003	1st	Birgit Prinz	Germany	1. FFC Frankfurt
	2nd	Mia Hamm	United States	Washington Freedom
	3rd	Hanna Ljung-berg	Sweden	Umeå IK
2004	1st	Birgit Prinz	Germany	1. FFC Frankfurt
	2nd	Mia Hamm	United States	Washington Freedom
	3rd	Marta	Brazil	Umeå IK
2005	1st	Birgit Prinz	Germany	1. FFC Frankfurt
	2nd	Marta	Brazil	Umeå IK
	3rd	Shannon Boxx	United States	Ajax of Los Angeles
2006	1st	Marta	Brazil	Umeå IK
	2nd	Kristine Lilly	United States	KIF Örebro DFF
	3rd	Renate Lingor	Germany	1. FFC Frankfurt
2007	1st	Marta	Brazil	Umeå IK
	2nd	Birgit Prinz	Germany	1. FFC Frankfurt
	3rd	Cristiane	Brazil	VFL Wolfsburg

WORLD PLAYER
OF THE YEAR
AWARD

YEAR	PLACE	PLAYER	NATIONALITY	CLUB
2008	1st	**Marta**	Brazil	Umeå IK
	2nd	**Birgit Prinz**	Germany	1. FFC Frankfurt
	3rd	**Cristiane**	Brazil	Linköping Corinthians
2009	1st	**Marta**	Brazil	Los Angeles Sol Santos
	2nd	**Birgit Prinz**	Germany	1. FFC Frankfurt
	3rd	**Kelly Smith**	England	Boston Breakers
2010	1st	**Marta**	Brazil	FC Gold Pride Santos
	2nd	**Birgit Prinz**	Germany	1. FFC Frankfurt
	3rd	**Fatmire Bajramaj**	Germany	Turbine Potsdam
2011	1st	**Homare Sawa**	Japan	INAC Kobe Leonessa
	2nd	**Marta**	Brazil	Western New York Flash
	3rd	**Abby Wambach**	United States	magicJack
2012	1st	**Abby Wambach**	United States	
	2nd	**Marta**	Brazil	Tyresö FF
	3rd	**Alex Morgan**	United States	Seattle Sounders Women
2013	1st	**Nadine Angerer**	Germany	1. FFC Frankfurt Brisbane Roar
	2nd	**Abby Wambach**	United States	Western New York Flash
	3rd	**Marta**	Brazil	

BIBLIOGRAPHY

I USED A wide variety of sources while writing *For Soccer-Crazy Girls Only*: websites, magazines, newspapers, books, and extensive interviews with current and former players and coaches.

Far and away, the most useful information came from spending time watching soccer and talking to people who love the sport and have spent their whole lives learning about the great game.

In case you'd like to do further reading on your own, this is a limited bibliography of the nonfiction books I found most interesting in my research:

Borden, Sam. *The Complete Idiot's Guide to Soccer Basics*. New York: Alpha Books, 2009.

Doyle, John. *The World is a Ball: The Joy, Madness, and Meaning of Soccer*. New York: Rodale Books, 2010.

Goldblatt, David. *The Ball Is Round: A Global History of Soccer*. New York: Riverhead Trade, 2008.

———. *The Soccer Book: The Sport, the Teams, the Tactics, the Cups*. New York: DK Publishing, 2009.

Hamm, Mia. *Go for the Goal: A Champion's Guide to Winning in Soccer and Life*. New York: HarperCollins, 1999.

Paige, Kerrie. *Soccer for Moms: Game & Parenting Essentials for Healthy Kids*. East Petersburg, PA: Fox Chapel Publishing, 2011.

St. John, Warren. *Outcasts United: An American Town, a Refugee Team, and One Woman's Quest to Make a Difference*. New York: Delacorte Books, 2012.

Watt, Tom. *A Beautiful Game: The World's Greatest Players and How Soccer Changed Their Lives*. New York: HarperCollins, 2010.

ABOUT THE AUTHOR

ERIN SODERBERG DOWNING is a lifelong soccer fanatic. She has written more than twenty-five books for kids and young adults. She is the author of the Quirks series and the forthcoming Puppy Pirates series (both written as Erin Soderberg), and also many funny, contemporary novels for tweens and teens. Before becoming an author, Erin was a children's book editor, a cookie inventor, and she also worked for Nickelodeon. She lives and writes (and manages her kids' soccer teams) in Minneapolis with her husband, three kids, and a soccer-crazy dog. More information about her books can be found at erindowning.com and erinsoderberg.com.

CREDITS

NOTES

NOTES

NOTES

NOTES

NOTES